G000096265

Counting Steps

a journey through landscape and fatherhood

MARK CHARLTON

INDEPENDENT INNOVATIVE INTERNATIONAL

Published by Cinnamon Press,
Meirion House,
Tanygrisiau,
Blaenau Ffestiniog,
Gwynedd
LL41 3SU
www.cinnamonpress.com

The right of Mark Charlton to be identified as author of this work has been asserted by him in accordance with the Copyright, Designs and Patent Act, 1988. © 2012 Mark Charlton. ISBN 978-1-907090-71-4

British Library Cataloguing in Publication Data. A CIP record for this book can be obtained from the British Library.

All rights reserved. No part of this publication may be reproduced, stored in a retrieval system, or transmitted in any form or by any means, electronic, mechanical, photocopying, recording or otherwise without the prior written permission of the publishers. This book may not be lent, hired out, resold or otherwise disposed of by way of trade in any form of binding or cover other than that in which it is published, without the prior consent of the publishers.
Designed and typeset in Garamond by Cinnamon Press. Cover design by Jan Fortune from original artwork Ancient Stepping Stones' by Bridget Jones © Bridget Jones, agency: Dreamstime.com,
Cinnamon Press is represented by Inpress and by the Welsh Books Council in Wales.
Printed in Poland
The publisher gratefully acknowledges the support of the Welsh Books Council.

Acknowledgments

I owe thanks to many people: to Jim Perrin for his unfailing encouragement; to Jane McNulty and Pat Borthwick for guiding me through a degree with the Open College of Arts; to all my friends at the Ty Newydd National Writing Centre and especially its director Sally Baker; to Ann Drysdale for her editing and Jan Fortune at Cinnamon Press for having faith.

But my greatest thanks are to Jane. Without her understanding and support this book would never have been possible. I love her dearly and hope I repay her in my way.

Contents

First steps — An Introduction

The essays in this book are a response to the delight I've found in fatherhood and landscape; to the people I love and the places I find myself returning. That much is straightforward, and if that were all, this introduction would scarcely be needed.

Ten years ago I was a painter, turning to writing only when my sketchbooks began filling with words. I quickly understood that though the crafts are different, they have similarities too – both require attention to truth, a looking inward as well as out, and a willingness to commit. This is where writing becomes especially difficult. For our true experience is more than the story of what happened where – and when that involves your family, it is tempting to hold back. I do so all the time.

There are elements of these essays that are deeply personal; self-revelatory to a level that feels uncomfortable. I'm conscious my wider family may be hurt by some of what I've written, particularly about my father – but I hope they will see the bigger picture. For ultimately this is a book inspired by joy, about the power of love and landscape; the ability to come through.

And it's important to remember that in writing we editorialise, developing a voice, which no matter how 'true' is only ever a part of us. I've never yet a met a writer who is not more complex (and flawed) than their work. These essays are no different: they draw from my life, but they are not an autobiography and should not be read that way.

Writing is a bittersweet passion. I work nearly always in Wales, at my house on the St David's peninsula: the place

I've come to love more than any other, where I feel most home. And yet I work alone, needing silence and space, distance from the very people I care about most. But it is they who dominate my thoughts, who give me strength and inspire me – without them the words would have no meaning.

For all they have given me:

Jane

Daniel (b. 1995)

Michael (b. 1996)

Dylan (b 2004)

Counting Steps

I suppose you have to start somewhere.

That said, you wouldn't choose the car park below Cerrig Lladron as the most inspiring place to begin. Deep ruts in the mud make parking difficult, glass from shattered windscreens litters the ground; someone has set alight the information board. Its charred and jagged edges mirror the granite spikes that puncture the rounded peaks beyond. Daniel surveys the bleak moorland; he looks unconvinced.

The Preseli Hills have been a constant presence for the fifteen or so years I've lived in Wales, their gentle curves forming the backdrop to my garden. And yet, I have never walked the length of the main ridge. Perhaps that's because I live in Pembrokeshire, where all eyes are fixed on the coast, seldom registering the subtler possibilities that lie inland. Or perhaps it's because the ridge is available; its proximity leading to complacency so that before long any sense of urgency slipped away – it will be there tomorrow, next week, next year. Or maybe it's because the logistics are awkward. It's a long linear route, a drop off one day, a pick up the next – there are always softer options which provide enough excuse to assuage the mild sense of guilt.

I am thinking all this as I watch Daniel struggling with his rucksack, the straps flapping in the wind. It is ill packed and the weight of the load pulls him backward, but I resist the urge to rearrange it. He is thirteen and growing out of his body: his shoes three sizes bigger in a year, his trousers too short and his nose too large for his face. And yet his hair is wispy and frail, his skin all freckles, turning to spots.

He waits for me to lead over the stile, kicking his feet in a pool of petrol-streaked water that reflects the gathering clouds. But there is more to his awkwardness than the threat of rain. I'd spent most of the journey here ranting at him for smearing mud over the newly cleaned car. 'Teenage incompetence,' I'd called it – it's become a regular phrase in our house – '*Why can't he just think for once... I've half a mind to call it off...*' I'd muttered on like this, Daniel silent in the back, until in her beautifully gentle way, Jane had helped me let it go. 'Don't spoil your time with him,' she said, 'he wants so much for you to enjoy this walk.'

A few steps over the stile and you realise something fundamental about the Preseli Hills; they are a sponge. And in the warmer air of April that sponge is sodden and full to bursting. I step gingerly between the tussocks of marram grass, using some rotten logs as duck-boards to take me over the worst of the bog. Daniel walks straight through; ankle deep in the peat he loses a boot on his third or fourth step.

I look momentarily to the sky but say nothing as I come back to help.

He is standing on one leg, picking his boot out of the mire. I offer my arm as he struggles to replace it, but he tips sideward, and in so doing pulls me over too. I end up on top of him as his backside sinks into the water.

We pull each other upright, and I turn to go. 'Follow me from now on will you.'

'I'm sorry Dad.'

'I just wish you'd think a little. We've barely gone a hundred yards and you're soaking wet.'

'I know,' he says and comes to my side.

I rub his hat and pull it jokingly over his eyes to say it doesn't matter and we start over the tussocked moorland that covers the slopes of Foel Cwmcerwyn, the first peak of the ridge. The walking soon becomes easier, the drier ground allowing us to look beyond our next few footsteps. Daniel walks closely but alone in his thoughts, his pack nudging me off the narrow path. I don't want to push him away but I find the silence between us difficult, so I mention that the grass is looking dull and tired.

'That's because we are on the northern side of the mountain. The grass gets less sun up here.'

'I guess so,' I reply.

'If you think about it, those fields by the coast are beyond the shadow line of the mountain. And it's a different type of grass that grows this high, which is probably why the sheep only come here in summer.'

It was only meant as a casual remark, something to pass the time, but he continues unabated.

'And there was snow here last month, so that might affect the grass too. Did you know this is where the ice that once covered Britain ended; it was kilometres thick and the sea was much further away then? The beach at Abereiddy was once a forest.'

'How do you know all that?' I ask.

'I read about it,' he says matter-of-factly. 'And I like noticing things too. Look how the shape of the valley changes as it runs down to the sea. That's because the glaciers stopped right here.'

I pause and look across to the sweep of Cardigan Bay, the sea fading into a violet horizon. I'm thinking about everything he has said. Whether he's correct about the grass and the glaciers is beside the point; it's the intensity of it, the level of observation and the certainty of his knowledge that is so unexpected.

'You're a funny one – all those thoughts in your head, but you can't keep your feet dry.'

'It doesn't matter about my feet.'

He turns his hat to a jaunty angle and pulls a goofy smile. 'Look Dad – teenage incompetent having fun.'

Sometimes I look at Daniel and wonder where he has gone; my golden boy, born after years of struggle; who wouldn't be here were it not for the astonishing technology of IVF. Aged three he was the cheeky one, pulling faces in the family photos; aged six he was the leader of the schoolyard pack, captain of the 'super-team', a bundle of energy whose every move is watched and adored by his younger brother. By the time he was nine he was quieter – his school said he was a joy to teach. Aged eleven he's more withdrawn – nothing serious, just what you might call 'quiet and sensitive' – he reads a lot, buys a snake as a pet and jokes he's becoming nerd. As he grows older I love him all the more; but we seem to clash over the littlest of things. I sense a distance has grown between us; a distance that seems to widen no matter how hard we both try.

I'm conscious too that for the last three years I've spent the majority of my spare time with his younger brother, Michael. Michael, the quiet and taciturn one – his infant teacher once asked me if he liked her – turned out to be a precociously talented cyclist. Some weeks we are seldom apart: training, racing, driving to events around the country – comfortable in the long silences of hours spent in the car. Michael dominates my thoughts and my dreams, the pictures on my office wall. I'm aware of the imbalance and the drift from Daniel – yet I'm driven by a vicarious pleasure in Michael's extraordinary gift, enthralled by his success and, I know, using it as an excuse.

But it would be wrong to say I hadn't tried with Daniel. The times I've asked him to come kayaking or climbing, to go fishing because he'd mentioned he'd like to try; to go to the library even. Jane suggested I try letting him choose – anywhere he liked so long as it was just the two of us. We went to London Zoo; he wanted to see the reptiles – we spent hours looking at snakes and tree frogs. He said it was the best day he'd had that year. Would he like to go again? Not for a while, he said.

Jane says that Daniel is happy in himself; that we'll find the time and reason to bridge the gap one day. Except it doesn't close and I find myself ranting at him more and more; frustrated as much as anything, watching him grow up and away from me.

Until one day in February, a week before his thirteenth birthday, he asked me, 'Would you take me camping this spring; maybe go backpacking in the mountains, like you did when you were a teenager.'

We've reached the cairn at Foel Feddau, a jumble of standing stones on a promontory that rises above what would once have been the glacial moraine. Below us are the villages, the coves and beaches I know so well. They look different from this angle, but then so too do the mountains.

The Preseli Hills can seem out of place in Wales. The greater part of them is rounded moorland, more akin to the Pennines or my childhood home of Northumberland. From a distance, and especially from the south, they look dull. And yet, up close, much of them is unexpected; their bleak expanses are punctuated by erratic pinnacles that give a feeling of bigger mountains, offering possibilities you had not considered. Their closeness to the coast makes them different too: showers scurry past quickly here – the rain tastes of salt – flashes of colour streak the bleached moors as the light reflects off the sea. The more I have come to know them the greater it seems is their capacity to surprise and delight.

I offer Daniel a drink. He questions if we'll have enough for our camp but I reassure him there will be a stream. He gulps at the bottle and I drain the last few drops.

Our next objective is Carn Menyn. I show him the map and explain that from where we are it is about three kilometres away.

'Except we have to go uphill,' he says. 'So it's further than on the map.'

I must have looked puzzled.

'Think about it,' he explains. 'The grid on a map assumes everything is flat. But if you go uphill you are travelling quite a bit further.'

'I'm not sure about that Daniel.'

'It must be. It's like a right-angled triangle; the hypotenuse is the longest side and that's what going up a mountain is like – it's further than along the bottom.'

As we walk on I ponder his theory with a sneaking suspicion that he's correct, aware that for all the years I've walked in the mountains I've never thought of this before.

I ask him if he has been learning about maps at school.

'No – but I was thinking about it before we came. I was wondering why maps of the world make Greenland look huge when on a globe it's much smaller. That's when I figured out how grids work'

'You think a lot, don't you?'

'Like you.' He sends me a wry glance. 'Just about different things.'

'I suppose so.'

'Thinking's good,' he declares.

We walk close together, silently now, past the rocks at Carn Bica and up the steeper climb leading to Carn Menyn.

As we approached the summit I notice he is counting his steps.

'Are you trying to measure the distance,' I ask? 'Because if you are, I think you were right about the up-hills being slightly longer than the map would suggest.'

'It's not that. I was counting so I'd know how far it was if we had to return in the dark.'

'You're a strange boy Daniel,' I tease.

'I know,' he replies, shrugging his shoulders and smiling.

It is late afternoon.

The rocks at Carn Menyn cluster in heaps at the base of a rough crag, the larger ones standing as upright pillars, the smaller ones scattered across the plateaux; cairns and stone circles, the work of new-age druids and spirit seekers, litter the hillside beyond. He asks why they have been built here.

I explain that these are the Bluestones; it was from here that pillars were taken to Stonehenge, dragged south to the Daugleddae estuary, and then taken by sea before their overland journey to what is now Salisbury Plain. The Bluestones make up the inner ring of the famous stone circle; they are overshadowed by the megaliths at the outer edge, but their journey was longer and in many ways more amazing to comprehend. I tell him, that a few years ago a group of archaeologists attempted to re-enact the journey, bringing a single stone from here to Wiltshire using only manpower. It took them three weeks to drag it to Milford Haven.'

'What happened then?'

'It sank the raft.'

He laughs. 'You'd have had a good rant about that, Dad!'

*

We climb down from the crags and decide to pitch our tent in the lee of the crag.

Daniel is interested in the process, asking me why the tent is shaped as it is; how do the poles work, shouldn't we pitch it end on to the wind? He unpacks his bag, examining the equipment I have bought him; laying out his mat, then mine, assembling the stove and busying himself around the camp. I watch him, not interfering, and reflect on the contrast to his brother who has the casual expectation that any assistance will simply appear. As he unpacks the food, Daniel reminds me that we'll need to find some water.

I look on the map to locate the nearest stream. Only one is marked, down a steep valley, about a kilometre to the south. There is a choice of routes: picking a way across the heather and grass or a clamber over rough boulders that I reckon has high potential for snapping ankles. I head off across the moor; Daniel chooses the rocks. Within a hundred yards my feet are soaked and sweat is pouring from me as I flail through the bog. Meanwhile Daniel is skipping over the boulders shouting directions and scouting ahead.

After twenty minutes of struggling I make it across to Daniel but there is no sign of the stream. I flop onto a boulder, my heart pounding, and steady myself to think. The sun is low in the sky.

'I'm sorry Dan, we'll have to go down. We can't camp here without water.'

He shrugs disconsolately and turns to look at the coast.

'I can't help it,' I snap. 'Have you got a better idea?'

'Listen,' he says, holding his finger to his lips. 'I can hear something.'

There is a trickle beneath us.

He grabs the water bottles and searches for holes between the boulders. I realise that the rocks he has been walking over are actually the dried up bed of the stream.

'It's too far underground,' I say.

He sticks his head down a hole. 'I think I can reach it.'

'It will be full of peat.'

There is a muffled reply as he burrows underground, his feet pedalling the air as he squeezes his body through the gap. I hold his legs steady as he wriggles inward.

'Pull me up,' he calls.

I tug on his boots and fall sideways as he jerks himself out of the hole, my backside hitting the ground with a squelch.

I am cursing at my indignity as he emerges, holding aloft two bottles of clear spring water.

'Teenage competence,' he says and grins.

By the time we return to the tent it is almost evening. We cook some pasta and soup before climbing to the summit of the rocks to watch the sun dip into the sea. All around us the stones are bathed in the ochre light, casting shadows across the slopes. There are dun coloured birds flitting among the cairns and we discuss what species they might be.

'I think the ones with white bums are wheatears,' I say. 'Those little ones are stonechats, or maybe rock pipits.'

'How do you know?'

'Your Grandad told me about the wheatears — he said they used to be called white-arses, but he was probably joking. I know about the others from books, and from years of looking, I guess. When I was your age I used to go searching for moths and butterflies.'

'Like those nights you took me hunting for owls and badgers — before Michael did his cycling.'

I recall our nocturnal trips and am washed over with a sense of guilt. I remember Daniel's delight at staying up late – how Michael never wanted to go – and how he loved the suspense of the hunt, his joy when we spotted an owl. It seems a long time ago.

'I've been thinking that maybe I spend too much time with Michael. If you and I did more things together we might disagree less. I'm sorry I get so ratty at times.'

'Mum says it's because you're like me underneath.'

'And what do you think?'

'I think it's all right you doing stuff with Michael. I mean, he's going to be a champion isn't he.'

'Perhaps.'

'Well it seems to me you should help him with that. But it would be good to do more walking up here.'

'And do you think we're very alike?'

He points to a long shadow that the crag is casting over the side of the mountain 'Do you see the outline of those two pinnacles?'

'Yes.'

'They aren't pinnacles at all,' he says. 'They are our shadows. If I wave my arm you can see it moving. It's as if we are part of the mountain.' He takes the camera out of his pocket. 'I want to take a photo for you.'

After he's taken some snaps we sit and watch the sun drop below the curving horizon. Across the valley the lights of isolated farms begin to flicker against the blackening hills. Stars appear.

'Do you think owls come up here?' he asks.

I doubt it. There are very few in the valley now.'

'I like the idea of being an owl,' he says, 'or a bat.' He makes a strange clicking noise with his tongue. 'Imagine what their world must be like – they see things by making noises and listening to the echo.'

'I'm not sure I'd call that seeing.'

'It is. They just do it differently to us. Lots of animals are like that: flies have hundreds of eyes; dogs can't see colours; some snakes are blind but they smell their prey.'

'Imagine being a mole,' I say. 'Living all your life underground and eating nothing but worms.'

'Or a beetle' he retorts. 'You spend years as a grub and then someone comes along and squashes you.'

'Or a moth; spiralling round what turns out to be candle.'

We laugh on our way back down the path. Daniel leads the way with my hand on his shoulder. And as we near the tent, I find myself counting steps in the dark.

The Nyfern

The Avon Nyfern is one of the shortest Welsh rivers to reach the sea. It springs from the glacial marsh at the foot of the Preseli Hills; in less than ten miles and two oxbow bends it has flattened into the most beautiful of Pembrokeshire's estuaries.

Despite its brief length the river does not want to hurry. Nowhere is it steep or straight, it's course a series of delays and diversions, as if reluctant to meet the incoming tide. By the time it reaches the hamlet of Nevern the river is bubbling over gravel beds and fishermen cast flies on its gentle current.

Nevern is a magical place. The churchyard has the best Celtic cross in Wales, an eleventh century masterpiece of interweaving curves. There's an Ogam stone too, and yew trees with bleeding sap and peculiar headstones with rhyming poetry. Over 140 wild flowers have been recorded in the graveyard.

From Nevern to the estuary is an awkward walk, the path, like the water, is reluctant to take you directly. But I have followed the river here, passing the pilgrim's cross that is hewn in the cliff, and the sand banks where the water eddies and otters leave their footprints, though I've never seen one. Eventually you reach the bridge at Newport where the tide and river meet.

It is about a mile to the sea from the bridge, but the flow is imperceptible. The tide becomes the dominant force and when low it reveals a broad mudflat that is one of the richest habitats for birds in West Wales. Now little egrets are established here, looking foreign beside the herons and crows, usually keeping their distance. The last time I was there I watched a turnstone, stilting by the waters edge, probing the mud in a leisurely fashion.

We first came here when the boys were toddlers. There's a graded track on the southern bank of the estuary that's perfect for pushing buggies. Despite its being fifteen miles from my house, we would make the effort to come, walking to the Parrog at the river's mouth, where there's a boat house and coffee shop and enough to divert the attention of little ones before they run the last few yards to the waves.

Even here it seems the river is reluctant. At low tide it flows in a deep channel between cliff and sand bar, forcing sailors to take a circuitous course to the Cat Rock, before finally the open sea. I've often seen boats caught on the sandbanks, waiting for the tide to rise, or revving engines to pull free before it falls.

Those stuck most often are the holidaymakers; visitors from the south and east that I unreasonably dislike – for in truth, they are not so different from me. Except they appear to learn nothing from the river: they are impatient to be moving, unsettled by the stillness and at odds with the flow.

Push, Pull Through

My feet ache from the climb.

Jane slumps down and swigs from the water bottle, her face is flushed, her boots dusty from the limestone path.

'You alright?' I ask.

She doesn't reply.

'Where are the boys?'

She points towards the small lake and I see them playing by the reed beds. Daniel is splashing in the shallows; Mike throws a rock into the pool.

'I didn't expect it to be so steep,' she says, passing me the water.

'The sign said it was only ninety minutes' walk.'

'For a mountain goat maybe.' She takes back the bottle before I've drunk and swigs the last few drops.

We've climbed to a crescent of five peaks that rise above the lac de Peyre, jagged spires of sienna earth, streaked with red. Jane is panting. I put an arm round her shoulder but she moves it away, though not with annoyance.

I lie back and breath deeply, feeling the beat of my heart, the taste of the earth in my mouth. A line of climbers makes their way through a boulder field that shimmers in the heat. I can hear cars grinding their way up to the Col de Grand Colombier, where we started this morning. Two eagles fly overhead.

As they approach I realise they are not eagles but lammergeyers, huge vulture that were reintroduced to these valleys a few years ago. One disappears over the peaks. The other glides in tighter and tighter circles until it is directly above us and I can barely see it for the glare of the sun. It swoops, as if to land, but at the last moment curls its wingtip and carves a perfect arc to the ridge.

'Did you see that?' I say.

Jane has her head between her knees.

'Are you sure you're alright?'

The boys are playing in the chalet garden and I'm sitting on the balcony watching the cable car make its way up the mountain. It's a little cooler in the shade but still no wind. There must be twenty paragliders circling the summit.

'Mark!' Jane calls me from the bathroom. I close my eyes a moment, too tired to move.

'MAAARK!'

I open the door and she is sitting on the toilet, damp from the shower that is still running. Her face is streaked with tears and she is holding a swatch of paper. It is stained with blood.

I'm instantly numb, my mind turning over possibilities in milliseconds. I can't think what to do, so I smile – a nervous reaction. *Think of something to say, Mark; think of something to say…*

'Perhaps it's just some spotting.'

She looks away. *Useless, ridiculous thing to have said.*

She stands up and I can see the crimson water in the bowl, more swatches of toilet paper stuck to the side. Her legs are running with blood.

'You'll need to see a doctor.'

'Not here,' she says, 'I don't want the boys to know.'

'But what about the baby?'

'It's gone. I know it has.'

I'm searching for a solution but there is none I can find. *Come on Mark, solutions are what you do, what you're best at.* It flashes through my mind that we won't need the extra bedroom; perhaps we can go on holiday this autumn. *What am I thinking?* I feel cold. *Think of something to say...*

'We'll go home tomorrow.'

'No,' she says, 'I couldn't stand it.'

She puts on a thin blue dressing gown and as I put my arms round her she begins to cry. Her body shakes as she gulps the air in short rapid breaths. The robe feels wet; it is the one she always packs, the one she wore when Daniel was born.

I hold her and the sobs merge slowly to a moan, then louder – as she digs her nails in my arm – into a single, visceral scream.

The road switchbacks ahead of me and I push hard on the pedals, rising out of the saddle to ease the stiffness in my legs. Jane is resting in bed. *'You go and ride your bike,'* she'd said, *'The boys will be fine.'* I only half protested.

I pass the charred timbers of a chalet that was hit by lightning last winter. It stands, black and twisted, at the end of the village, like some sort of outcast; we laughed when the boys nicknamed it *'chalet brulée'* I'd thought being hit by lightning was a chance in a million, but I'm told there are many strikes here each year.

The road steepens and sweat runs onto my face. I change up a gear, forcing myself into a new rhythm, but it's not enough. I change up again. I don't want a steady climb; I want to gasp for breath and for my legs to scream with pain; I want to feel sick from the effort; I want my senses alert; I want to feel alive and elated and aching all one and the same. And I want it to come quickly.

Always, with me, there is this ability to cut myself off, to close down emotions. Ability? I'm not sure I should call it that. It's what's expected of me though; what I expect of myself in a way. Mark will sort it out, they say, and usually I do.

I push harder and the more it hurts, the more the memories return.

The phone rang.
She drew her knees to her chin, and watched me as I answered.

'It's Bourn Hall Clinic. We have the results of your IVF treatment…'

And when I told her she screamed then too. She cried for over an hour. I tried to tell her what they'd said about the tests and the data, and how she had to go back to Cambridge to have a scan, and how she'd need special drugs to help the foetus along. But she wasn't listening. It could wait she said.

'You can cry too,' she said. 'We're going to have a baby.'

There's a flatter section now; dead straight for a kilometre before the hairpins begin. I can see our chalet from here, the boys are playing in the garden, chasing each other with the butterfly nets.

Last night, a hawkmoth flew to the terrace as we ate dinner. Mike kept trying to grab it. But each time it would dart away, only to return a few minutes later, entranced by the scent of the nectar. Daniel watched intently as it hovered over the table, gently unfolding its proboscis into the trumpets of the flowers. He looked so beautiful, his head cupped in his hands, watching this amazing creature, not saying a word.

It took us four years of trying before Daniel was born.

At first, when her periods kept coming, we laughed about it. 'We need to do it more often,' I'd say. But after a while Jane said the jokes weren't funny.

So the consultations began: the tests, the investigations, the year on Clomid *(or was it two?)*; more investigations, drugs, specialists, operations, some hope, soon gone, then cold jokes - then despair.

And then the prospect of IVF and trips across the country and faint hope growing again and Jane driven like never before; more tests, more drugs, thousands of miles in the car, never a complaint from her, me worrying about the cost, and her mother half interfering but not quite...

A year later Daniel arrived.

One was enough, I said.

Three months after Daniel was born I returned from a business trip abroad. I remember Jane was waiting for me in the lounge and the first thing she said was

> *'I'm pregnant again.'*
> *'You can't be...'*
> *'I am. Honestly, I am.'*
> *But she was only half smiling.*
> *'Are you annoyed?' she asked.*

And I remember standing there after she left the room and wondering why she thought I might be annoyed?' True, Daniel was a difficult baby – bloody difficult. But then the whole process had been difficult.

I scarcely remember her being pregnant that second time, or even Mike as a baby. There was so much happening; it was enough to get from day to day. I couldn't understand those men who said the birth of their children was the best moment of their life. Truth was, I didn't believe them. I remember saying, 'Our life's on hold while they grow up.'

Yet as they grew I found myself pulled, as if by gravity, into ever-deeper love and concern. At first I barely noticed, but its grip slowly tightened until I'd find myself waking at night and worrying they'd choked, or fallen, or worse. And I'd get up to check even though I knew it was irrational, and stand and watch them sleeping, their arms intertwined like those golden figures in the paintings of Klimt. And afterwards, I'd lie awake and try not to think about the day they'll leave home, as they surely will – feeling sick at the thought – until my heart slowed and the dread faded.

I read somewhere that if you fell into a black hole you'd pass through an imperceptible moment, an 'event horizon', beyond which struggle would be pointless. It was something like that.

I'm at the hairpins; ten corners to the top, each one numbered in my mind, each one harder than the last. An elderly couple are sitting by the road, playing cards at a table laid with a chequered cloth and wine glasses; their motor home is parked in the lay-by behind.

'*Allez! Allez!*' They clap me as I pass and I stand on the pedals to drive them a hard as I can. The technique takes time to learn. It's important not only to push, but also to pull through at the end of each stroke. The pull takes the leading pedal over a point of no return, so your weight can force it down with enough momentum to pull through again. *Push; pull through.* Think of how a bull stamps its hooves.

Mike was a one off, they said. The IVF drugs had suppressed Jane's immune system. We'd been lucky to a have a second child; it wouldn't happen again, they said. So that was it for seven years. Barely a thought from me, though always, I knew, a yearning from Jane.

Until last year. Her joy all the greater for the surprise, my own tempered by practical concerns; everyone telling us we'd need an extra bedroom, as if we didn't know; the boys excited but with no real understanding.

A month later, the bleeding had started. It was Christmas Eve.

'Miscarriage is very common in women your age.' The consultant was very matter of fact, 'There are drugs that can help if we'd known your history...'

We left the ward on Christmas morning and Jane had buried her face in my shoulder as a dozen heads turned silently to watch.

My legs stiffen as I round the bend by the Chalet Vernier. I pull on the bars for leverage, my fingers numb from gripping too tightly. The crescent of peaks glow pink in last of the light. *Keep pushing; pull through.* The path we took this morning a scar on the mountain.

A shadow moves across the cliffs. It is the lammergeier, soaring in the same tight circles as this morning.

The road is painted with slogans: Go Lance, Vivre Virenque, Allez Confidis. Next week the Tour de France will traverse this pass. There are dozens of vans up the road, parked at odd angles, perched on the edge of cliffs. A group of campers watch me as I pass, gauging my speed. A woman bangs her spoon on the table and a couple of the men clap half-heartedly. I smile, unable to raise my hand, but already they are looking down the road for the next rider.

There are more names on the tarmac: Basso, Salvoldelli, Ulrich. *She should have asked for some drugs. How many of the riders will have taken something to help them along? Who cares – who the fuck cares?*

My eyes are wet. I wipe them with the back of my hand, but they fill again. *Push; pull through.* I can feel the breeze coming over the col. *We should never have walked so far today.* The computer tells me I'm doing six miles an hour. *It was too hot; too steep.* I dig my nails into my palms and blood runs on the bars. *The swatches of paper in the bowl.* I want to throw up from the effort. *The boys running inside when she cried...*

I've reached the col.

That single, visceral scream

A woman is standing by the side of the road. She is staring at me and I realise that I'm screaming too. Screaming at the mountain; at the lammergeyer, as it glides towards the peak.

Thin rivers are running down my cheeks. I wipe them away but they flow doesn't stop.

I can taste my tears.

For Dylan

Five years. Has it really been that long?

It feels like yesterday and forever. So much life in such a short time.

Time Passes. Tick-tock, Tick-tock...

So wrote Dylan Thomas, after whom you're named. I wished you his genius if not his weakness. You have his charisma already, and his bombastic ways – you sing like a Welshman too! But I forgive you your faults, as I always will.

Strangely, I can't remember your birth, perhaps because it was so early in the morning. What I do recall is bringing you home. And your brothers sitting on the bed; looking not touching, just as they were told – then gently, one at a time, holding your hand. They wanted you to wake, but you slept through it all, oblivious.

Oblivious too of the years of yearning, the three miscarriages, the nuchal scans, the waiting for results, the tests and more tests – and the waiting – always more waiting – until the final phone call. And when it came, the nurse asked if I was sitting down.

'All clear,' she said.

You see that's the thing about probability – it doesn't work in the real world. There is only one you and you were always perfect. Just like there's no probability or quantum for love: you either do or you don't; all or nothing, no half-measures. And every day you remind me of that simple, inexpressible, fact.

Happy birthday Dylan; it's the least and the most I can say.

The Teifi

The Teifi estuary is, I always feel, an inauspicious start to the Pembrokeshire Coast Path. Poppit Sands is little more than a jumble of car parks, a concrete lifeboat station and a wooden cafe that is seldom open. The 'sands' themselves are grey, darkened by shale and tidal mud, chief collection point for the flotsam of Cardigan Bay.

And beyond, up the steep lane that leads to the Youth Hostel (like a three-bed-semi with picture windows) it is little better. The farmyards are littered with tyres, the hill cottages colonised by putative eco settlers, their ubiquitous wind-catchers flapping on every gatepost. Looking to the north, the view of Cardigan Island is sullied by the hotels and caravan sites that pepper the shoreline.

I have never liked it much here. There is not enough space for the river to end and the sea to begin; it is more of a harbour's mouth than an estuary proper. The Teifi has carved a deep channel between silted banks, allowing boats to sail up river at virtually all tides. Cardigan, despite giving its name to the great sweep of Mid-Wales coastline, is actually four miles inland.

In fact the river is more impressive by the town, above which it flattens into an expanse of wetland, home to otters, warblers, herons and recently, a bittern. Upstream is the fabulous Cilgerran gorge, then Cenarth with its water mill (I once saw a seal here); further up is the fairy glen of Henllan falls and the seemingly innocuous weir that has taken the lives of too many kayakers – one of them someone I knew well. Many years ago I helped in a small way to establish the canoe centre at Llandysul; soon afterwards, the 'safe' slalom course I'd paddled dozens of times would take another life.

As we walked down the Teifi estuary this week I urged Daniel on. I wanted to put the river behind me, to reach Cemaes Head and watch the Kestrels on Pen yr Afr before the light began to fade. We'd half planned to camp out, but it's difficult here. The cliffs are high and sloping, the path traverses at half height and there are few places to sit never mind pitch a tent. It began to rain.

We pressed on to Ceibwr, climbing the highest section of the coast path, passing the ravens nests at Foel Hendre as the wind licked up a downpour. By the time we reached Trewyddel it was almost dark, the car wouldn't start and the road was running like a stream.

Eventually the engine turned.

We headed for home, the last of the light smothered by the thickening clouds.

Moth Hunt

As teenagers, my brother and I used to catch moths on summer nights. We had home-made nets from bamboo poles and lace curtains, the design copied from those we'd seen in the catalogues of Watkins and Doncaster: *The Naturalist*.

You'd never see it now: two boys in duffle coats, out at midnight, carrying jam jars and oversize fishing nets, lurking under streetlights and looking for tell-tale flickers in the shadows.

There was one particularly good spot, by a patch of wasteland near the railway station. To reach it we would walk down a narrow unlit path, bounded on its right by a brick wall that cast long shadows over beds of nettles and bramble. Into the gloom lay a wilderness of Willow Herb, Convolvulus and Hawthorn – food-plants, we thought, of the elusive and desirable Elephant Hawk Moth. Above the station doors a small bulkhead light cast a faint glow, attracting dozens of moths that spiralled endlessly in its beam.

Fast-forward thirty years and I am standing in a queue outside Kempton Racecourse with my two sons tugging at my sleeves. The line snakes ahead for a good 100 yards. Next to me is a man in a tweed jacket and dusty brogues, a stout woman with a felt hat, a teenager in a tee-shirt with a scorpion motif. There is a chap with a large wooden box under each arm and a rucksack on his back. His companion, who is carrying a stack of photographs, has hitched his trousers so high they stop four inches short of his shoes.

'I've brought the *lifecycle* shots,' says the man with the photos to his friend.

'They make a fine show,' the man with the rucksack tells me, flashing an enormous set of teeth. 'You must come and see it, wonderful shots of odonata.'

'What's odonata?' whispers Daniel.

'Dragonflies,' I explain.

'Are they mini-beast?'

'Sort of,' I say, and I raise my eyes at the man with the teeth as if to excuse him.

He tells the boys they should join the Bug Club if they want to know more about dragonflies. 'Can we?' they plead.

'If you like,' I consent.

The man stoops down saying not to miss the displays on the upstairs gallery – there are lots of mini-beast up there.

Daniel asks if he can have a scorpion.

Mike says he wants, 'One of those big moths like Dad has in the loft.'

Our trip to the loft is why we are here.

They have a school project on insects so I'd suggested, 'Let's go on a moth hunt,' and the three of us are soon crawling trough the hatch at the top the stairs with a flickering torch. 'I wonder what's in here?' I say, opening a chest I'd sealed twenty years previously – they shriek with delight when I show them the moths pinned to pieces of cork in old cigar boxes.

My childhood floods back with each lid that's opened: moths and butterflies, beetles, stick insects. The labels are still intact, handwritten scribbles beneath crumbling specimens. In one box there's an atlas moth that we hatched from a cocoon, it's about eight inches in span. In another, an Elephant Hawk and a label that reads, *Railway Station, Whitley Bay, 1974.*

Jane wants nothing to do with it; she says nobody kills insects anymore. Daniel replies that's not true: there's a machine in Sainsbury's that zaps flies, and anyway, Miss Garton told them about farmers who use sprays to kill bugs. At bedtime Mike quizzes me on how to catch butterflies, what's the biggest moth in the world and whether they feel it when you put the pin in. I show them an old book I'd found in the chest and tell them how, years ago, a man gave it to me at a special insect show.

'Can we go there too?' asks Daniel.

I'm not sure who likes the idea the most.

I do a quick search on Google and a week later we're at what the programme says is the largest insect fair in Europe – the annual exhibition of the Amateur Entomologists' Society.

It's starting to rain and the crowd is trying to shelter under the canopy. Somebody knocks over a shopping trolley, spilling jars and boxes down the steps – people push towards the entrance. 'Steady, gentlemen,' says a military voice.

The doors open and we are carried inside as the crowd jostle and shove to be first at the stalls.

'Don't go far,' I call as the boys head off. 'and remember, Mum said not to buy anything that's alive!'

I am standing by the doors looking in at the hall. It is like a jumble sale by Indiana Jones: tables piled with breeding cages, butterfly nets, moth traps, and displays of what look like surgical instruments. I've lost sight of the boys. Over each table there are banners with the names of the dealers: Classey's Books, World of Nature, Atropos Cabinets, Watkins and Doncaster: The Naturalists.

I want to laugh; I can't believe they're all still here.

I must have been thirteen. It seems astonishing now that my parents allowed me and my brother to catch the overnight train from Newcastle to London? We had Saveloy sandwiches in the cafe at the station and thought it very grown up. I wanted to meet a man called Robert Godden. He owned a butterfly farm and I'd written to him on best blue writing paper, asking how I might become a 'professional entomologist'. I can still remember his business address: Worldwide Butterflies, Over Compton, Sherbourne, Dorset. A few years ago I went to look it up – it had closed, the buildings abandoned, the garden and polytunnels overgrown. I remember he told us that he was quite famous, because he was trying to save the Large Blue from extinction but it would take years to repair the damage. He'd written a book – *The All Colour Book of Butterflies* – the one I'd showed to the boys last week.

Daniel pulls at my arm. He's found the scorpions. Can he have one?

I remind him what his Mum said.

He screws his face, 'Aw, D-a-a-d.'

'Not a scorpion anyway.'

'So what can we have?' he jumps on the hint of weakness.

'We'll see.'

A man pushes past me to the table on my right. He's peering at a case of enormous green butterflies. '*Papilio antimachus*?' he asks the dealer, 'Captive bred, I suppose – you wouldn't have any that are wild-caught would you?'

'The stewards would close me down.' The dealer glances round the hall before adding, 'I have some round the back that I couldn't possibly display, if you know what I mean.'

A grey haired woman is looking at the same case. She has a magnifying glass at her eye. The man interested in the *antimachus* is trying to edge past, but she won't budge.

'I think there are mites in this case,' she announces.

'There are not!' the dealer retorts, flushing.

She ignores him and turns to me, offering her glass. 'What do you think?' I suppress a smile and say I'm sorry but I have to find my boys.

By now the dealer is red in the face, 'There are *definitely* no mites in my cases!'

I edge slowly through the throng, spot the boys at the next table and grab the hoods of their coats.

'It's good to see the youngsters here,' says a man from Insects Direct.

'Yes,' I reply, keeping a tight hold of Mike to stop him prodding a cage of mantises.

'Teenagers are only interested in the exotics,' he says ruefully. 'A bit of pond dipping at the weekends was all we needed.'

'Quite,' I reply, not knowing how else to answer.

'Here, you can have these for free.' He hands the boys each a plastic tub with a large insect inside. 'They've lost their antennae,' he explains.

'He's given us scorpions,' says Daniel. 'Mine's the biggest,' and he holds up the tub to show me a six-inch creature with a curled tail.

'It's a stick insect,' I say,' *eurycantha calcarata*.' The dealer looks impressed and I'm amazed at my own dredged memories.

'I'm going to call him Terry the Terrible,' says Daniel.

'But it's a lady stick insect.'

'Terry-lina,' cackles Mike, his face beaming. 'Mum will hate it.'

*

Upstairs the balcony is lined with exhibits. Here are passions as obscure as the sawflies of Hampshire, photographing plume moths, rearing larvae on agar solutions, and the decline of ground beetles and chafers. The man with the teeth is by his display of dragonfly photographs, there's a chap selling a self-published book: *Fangs for the memories – a guide to breeding tarantulas*. A lady showing a collection of stag beetles allows Mike to hold one; she uses Latin nomenclature with the ease with which they talk of Pokemon.

Mike is disappointed. He tells me that the beetles take five years to grow and live inside trees, so they won't make good pets.

'Your stick insects are better,' I console him.

'Can we really keep them?'

I kneel down and put my arms over their shoulders. 'Of course – but let me tell Mum.'

Dan gives me a hug. 'Can Harry come round to see them? He's got a lizard in his bedroom.'

I think of the cages in the room I shared with my brother – dozens of them, stacked to the ceiling. It was our secret world – friends were not allowed at the house. My father said it was a good hobby because it kept us quiet while he slept – or outside while he watched the racing. I'd spend long days writing lists and drawing diagrams in the library, collecting specimens from the old quarry or the sand dunes. I acquired a vast range of nerdy knowledge and I knew it was odd even then – but I didn't care.

Later I started to rear silkmoths, selling their eggs to collectors to raise pocket money - some of them were probably here. The idea of killing and pinning insects is frowned on nowadays, not in tune with our spirit of conserving nature, one up from birds nesting. It wasn't exactly fashionable then – but then it was never about collecting, or even the moths for that matter.

There's a roar as a plane coming into Heathrow passes over Sunbury. People are leaving the pavilion, arms full of boxes and books, there's someone pushing a cabinet on a sacking trolley. A family is eating a picnic by the parade ring; the father is ignoring the food but examining the beetles he has bought.

We make to leave through the hall and as we do, I notice a stall selling moth traps – the poster advertises, 'Designed by Robert Godden.'

'Need any help?' asks an elderly man with a thick Australian accent.

Of course, he was Australian!

'Just looking,' I reply, staring.

'Do you have a moth trap?' His voice the same after all this time.

'I had one as a boy,' I say, almost stuttering. 'I used go camping with it.'

'Then you'll be wanting one again.'

'I'm not sure,' I hesitate. 'It's thirty years since I...'

I'm wondering if I should say anything. I want to thank him, for showing an interest in a young boy, explaining about the Large Blue and how it takes time for damage to repair. But where do I start? Mike is leaning on my legs and I can sense he's flagging. So instead I ask the price of the traps.

'I'm retired,' he says. 'But I still come every year – it's in the blood I think. A hundred quid for the small ones – I'll throw in a net for your boys.'

'Dad's buying a moth trap,' Mike calls to his brother.

'It's not alive,' says Dan, 'So Mum can't mind about that.'

*

Driving home the boys are squabbling.

'Daniel's insulting me,' complains Mike. 'He keeps saying I'm a grub – he says his stick insect will bite me.'

I try to distract them, telling how I used to look for moths at midnight, by the alley near the railway station – how the bulkhead light captured them in its beam. We can take our new trap to the woods I suggest; maybe go camping – we might catch thousands.

'Can we have a moth party?'

'Of course,' I say, 'all your friends can come.'

'What are we going to say to Mum?'

'We'll think of something'

'She won't mind, will she Dad?'

'Of course not,' I reply. 'She understands.'

The Tywi

There was a time when I thought Carmarthen was the worst bottleneck in Wales – the hours I've spent behind tractors, devising rat-runs to avoid the tailbacks on bank holidays. It's a pointless exercise; to get east or west you have to cross the Tywi and there's only one bridge. Once I queued for two hours, only to find the A40 had been closed at St Clares! That was the first time I went to Llansteffan – to wait for things to clear.

This week we returned. It was raining and the car park at Tesco was so full they were queuing to get out. 'Everyone's stocking up,' said Jane, 'perhaps town will be better?' Forty minutes later and we're nose to tail on the bypass. 'There's no point getting angry,' she says, as I hit the horn and swing the car around.

Llansteffan is as good a place to wind down as any I know. It feels like a smaller, more lived in, version of Laugharne.

But whereas Laugharne is a disappointing place (were it not for the association with Dylan Thomas it would not merit its visitors) Llansteffan is surprising and about as unspoiled as they come. It also has a better castle, a proper beach, and an eccentric grocers-cum-bistro-cum-lodging house that would not be out of place in Under Milk Wood.

This is not to say that Llansteffan is pretty – its foremost charm is a sort of relaxed shabbiness that comes from ageing gracefully rather than primping up to fit the tourist pastiche. Its other charm is that it sits at the head of the Tywi.

The Tywi is the longest river to run its course entirely in Wales; rising in the Cambrian mountains it meanders through quiet valleys to Llandovery and Llandeilo, past castles and stately farms, before eventually reaching the sea below Carmarthen.

I say 'reaches the sea' as if there were a definite point, but in practice it isn't like that. At low tide the estuary stretches to the horizon, the water and land gradually dissolving into one another. We watched the tide turn from the ramparts of the castle – the pink sands blending to indigo, the water thickening more than flowing – and the distant hills of Gower the only discernible feature.

The castle stands above the village, at the end of a single-track road on the last spit of land; there are no signs and no parking allowed. The rain eased as we explored the keep and gatehouse, and as if in keeping with Llansteffan's capriciousness we stumbled on a gothic photo shoot – a girl in purple bodice and leather boots, shivering under an arch and losing her temper at a guy who was struggling with the flashlights.

As the tide began to race the channel that separates Llanstreffan from Ferryside on the opposite bank, widened. We watched a fishing boat that had slipped its mooring, drifting in the eddies, going nowhere it seemed.

The sky brightened but the wind stayed bitter; Jane returned to the car, leaving me with Dylan who'd wanted to play on the castle walls. He huddled close, pushing his tiny fingers into my mouth for warmth and comfort, sucking on his lips as he did so. The tide had caught the fishing boat and was carrying it upstream.

The traffic would have eased by now – it was time to go home.

Homage

'Let's start with some poetry,' he said.

He stood in the centre of the group, dressed all in black, and read from a battered blue notebook. His voice was louder than I'd expected, a little flat in tone. We listened intently, trying to fathom the meaning of the words.

> *He, standing hushed, a pace or two apart,*
> *Among the bluebells of the listless plain,*
> *Thinks, and remembers how he cleansed his heart*
> *And washed his hands in innocence in vain.*

He snapped the notebook shut.

'So what's all that about then?'

There was no reply.

He recited the poem again, this time from memory.

'The trouble is,' he said, 'If you think of it as a story it doesn't quite work. All of the words make sense, yet the meaning isn't clear in a traditional way.'

'It's beautiful though', said a girl who, I'd noticed, seemed to hang on his every word.

'Exactly,' he said. 'And I think if Housman had spelled out some sort of narrative, it wouldn't have worked. It was the feeling that mattered; the feeling he wanted to express and the feeling it gives us when we read it today.'

He turned to directly me.

'Now tell me,' he barked. 'How can you paint like Housman writes?'

This was my first introduction to John Skinner. I had come to a figure-painting course, recommended by the teacher of my local art class. I'd expected to find a studio with drawings on the walls, some easels, and perhaps a model waiting in a robe. I'd expected everyone to prepare quietly, sorting their pencils and charcoals, sneaking glances at each other's sketchbooks. And yet here we were discussing poetry with this strangely charismatic man, in a room that was bare, save for a few tables stacked against the walls.

John explained that we wouldn't have a model that first morning, instead we would paint from our imagination. Later, when the model arrived, she would walk amongst us so we didn't get stuck on a static image. He made us draw without looking, to paint straight onto canvas – *'no preparation, no hesitation'* – and on a scale I'd never before considered. He couldn't care less if I had any skill or not; I should forget all I'd learned about proportions and foreshortening. 'You're not here to copy objects,' he said. 'You're here to realise your sensations in paint.'

And there were none of the pleasantries of my weekly art class. The group of regulars, were expected to give detailed criticisms of each other's work. The comments were fierce. At one point, the girl who had looked so doe eyed at John, ripped up her drawings and began to cry. In the breaks the group discussed poetry and contemporary art with the same intensity as blokes arguing over football. There was an evangelical air to their fervour; and they were all, I decided, in awe of John.

I struggled that first weekend and yet I was captivated too, by John's passion, by the sheer force of his personality. I left with my head spinning and folder full of drawings.

When I got home, I showed some to Jane.

'What the heck are those?' she said.

*

Over the next eight years John Skinner would transform the way I viewed the world. He would become my friend, my tutor and mentor, a constant source of inspiration and a partner in ideas. He would teach me more about art than I had learned in twenty years of painting. It would never be easy. We would argue as much over trivial meanings as big issues; over his romanticism and his notions, as I called them; over my rationality and the failure of logic, as he would put it. With John there would always be combat, it came with the territory, so to speak. But our friendship would take us both to new places and different ways of seeing.

A few days after that first weekend, John phoned me. We had talked in the pub about my job as a strategist and how difficult it was to get people to see creative possibilities. I'd suggested he had something to offer in that field; was he phoning to follow up? He wasn't much interested in that conversation, he said. He wanted a marketing plan for his studio, and in return he would give me a free tutorial. I had potential, he said with disarming candour, providing I stopped going to evening classes.

We met at his studio-gallery and I began by asking to see his paintings. He was pleased; he'd met dozens of advisors from the Arts Council and the Small Business Service. 'All of them were crap. None of them looked at the paintings. I am hoping you might be different.'

'No pressure then,' I said.

'Of course there's pressure,' he replied. 'This is the most important thing in my life.'

I soon discovered just how difficult John could be. Almost every suggestion I made he dismissed. He wouldn't stock pottery or glass – '*I'm not selling trinkets*'. He would never use a London gallery again – '*bloody sharks*'. He wouldn't discount his paintings, even to regular buyers – *'they're a lifetime of ideas and they're not going cheap'*. When I described his racks of canvases as 'old stock', he almost exploded.

He wanted, he said, to make enough money to spend more time painting. He wanted to be less reliant on courses, to spend less time selling his work – to do less, it seemed to me, of anything that might make him some money. The work was all that mattered, he kept saying.

I was fascinated by his attitude. What appeared dogmatic was, I realised, a deep integrity. Impractical perhaps, but somehow compelling. I envied his determination to stick to what he believed, not to compromise for the sake of money. His approach to life felt like the opposite of mine. When I was eighteen I had given up painting to do a 'proper degree'. Later, as I came to love philosophy, I gave up a post-graduate scholarship to get a 'proper job'. My work since had been a pragmatic compromise – I was proud of what I had achieved and I fitted in time for my interests as and when I could. Yet as I talked to John, I felt as if I'd sold out cheaply. He had that effect on people.

I sent him a business plan the likes of which I'd never written before. It had no formal structure, simply dozens of ideas – most of which I knew he wouldn't accept. And I challenged his obstinacy; he couldn't expect the world to pay him to paint, just because he wanted to. But there were possibilities, and his personality was a vital ingredient. I told him his 'groupies' adored him – he should build on that. Like it or not, the 'Skinner factor' was his best chance of making big money.

He rang me up two days later. 'Fantastic plan,' he said. 'You're the first person to take this seriously.'

'You like the ideas?'

'God no, they're dreadful. But it's helped me see things differently. I've been faffing around; like you with your night classes. Come down again and let's talk about how we can make big money.'

The next time we met he had a video playing in the studio.

'Look at this,' he said. It was the band, Portishead, scratching records as the introduction to a song. ' When I was a kid we thought scratching a vinyl was bad; the worst thing you could do.' He fast-forwarded to a clip of Jimi Hendrix playing the guitar. 'In those days, musicians hated electronic feedback, and yet Hendrix realised he could use it.'

'I'm not sure what you're getting at,' I said.

'Hendrix saw it differently; he turned what people considered crap into something like gold. It's the same with scratching records – who first thought of that? It's like there's fine line between things being really bad and the opening up of new possibilities. I've been thinking about this a lot.'

He put on a clip of Eddie Izzard. 'Fashion goes in cycles,' said Izzard, drawing an imaginary circle in the air. 'It starts with dull, then normal, then cool, then hip and groovy'… Izzard paused and held his arm above his head before completing the circle… 'Then looking like a dick head.' The audience laughed. 'I like to cruise that back edge,' he joked. 'It makes me feel good, but sort of sick.'

'John, you've lost me,' I said.

'That's what I want from my paintings,' he said. 'I want them to make me feel good, but almost sick.'

'My paintings make me feel sick,' I replied, 'they are so bad at the moment.'

'That's because they aren't bad enough. You need to make them really dreadful – so they suggest a new way forward.'

'I can't do that.'

'Yes you can. You can do what you like,' he said. 'Your trouble is you won't take any chances.'

This conversation was typical of John, taking notions and spinning themes and variations, but never quite reaching a coherent outcome; not caring that he didn't. To me, who'd worked all my adult life in a target driven business, which measured success in sales and margins and gradual improvement, the idea of making something worse to make it better just didn't add up. Yet I sensed the possibilities. I knew also that he was right about playing safe. I was trading any real success for the safety of mediocrity and a little praise. Deep down I knew my paintings were pretty pale imitations of what I wanted them to be.

'I'm not sure people would understand,' I said.

'You've got to get used to ridicule, or at least risk it. When the work's good enough, the jokes will stop. And anyway, why do you care? It's not as if you need to sell your paintings is it?'

He was right again. It cost me more in materials and course fees than I made selling the odd picture. It was pleasing to know someone had bought them, but surely that wasn't why I wanted to paint?

'You need to think what you get from this, Mark. I wouldn't say that if it wasn't important.'

'I thought you wanted to talk about making big money.'

'I do,' he said. 'But I promised you a tutorial. Anyhow, it's the painting I care about most.'

As I looked round his studio I could see what he meant. He had a just finished a series of landscapes on the theme of air sea and hills. They were huge semi-abstract paintings on a scale and ambition that, to me, was overpowering. Nothing about these paintings was easy; some I quite liked, most I couldn't understand. But the aspiration behind them was clear. They were more than just paintings; as John might have put it, they were a way of connecting with something beyond him.

My own attempts at connecting resulted mainly in frustration. I tried painting with more expression, but I wasn't quite sure why. I tried 'painting my sensations', but ended up confused. I tried to use 'marks as a language' but found myself lost for words. Over the months that followed, I came slowly to realise that all the skills I had acquired (and I was a good painter in a conventional sense) were not much use for where I wanted to go. He was right about the ridicule though. Jane at least tried to understand; others thought I'd lost it completely.

Painting with John was no longer a pastime; it was an intense experience, a struggle in every sense. And each time I got frustrated, he'd encourage me to do more of the same.

'Make the paintings even worse,' he'd say. And I'd go off to try again, never quite making them bad enough.

Part of my problem was the lack of logic behind his method; I craved a clear explanation, but with John that was never easy to find. A bigger problem, through I didn't realise it at the time, was that I was trying to please him, and still not painting for myself.

It was year before a breakthrough came. As always, with John, it wasn't straightforward.

'I'm fed up with this,' I ranted, during one of our tutorials. By now I'd joined a group of regulars who he considered his more serious students.

Instead of the usual cajoling, he took me to the top of the hill outside his studio. We leant into the wind, the thin line of Chesil Beach far below us, waves dumping on the pebbles, fishermen casting lines past the surf. We had to shout over the stiffening breeze.

'I used to come here and tell myself I could never paint this.' He gestured to the sea, the horizon curving in an arc towards Lyme Bay. 'It was five years before I knew where to start.'

'How did you begin?'

'Someone came into the studio and started talking about swimming away from the shore. He said he was afraid of the shallows, because there wasn't enough water to hold him up.'

'I don't understand.'

'It doesn't matter; it just made me see it differently. It's not logical. I realised it was the weight of the sea that I felt – its depth and its power – and that's what I needed to paint.'

'Maybe, but all this painting your sensations – it's your way John, not mine. I feel like I want to paint straight lines, stripes even. That's what I really want to do.'

'So paint stripes. Maybe that's your true response.'

'But I can't just do that.'

'You can do whatever you like.'

When we returned to the studio he took a four-foot canvas from the rack and handed me a brush loaded with paint.

'Now paint your stripes,' he said, 'paint them now, before you lose the feeling.'

As I drove the brush across the canvas I felt a sense of relief, of joy. More than that, I felt that I was connecting to something beyond reason. Even now I don't quite have the words to describe it.

It had taken me a year of struggling to reach this point – the result was three vertical stripes, applied in less than thirty seconds. I remember standing back and admiring them, grinning even.

It felt like my best ever painting.

Gwaun

The Gwaun tends to be overlooked by tourists: there are no obvious attractions, the access is difficult and the villages are, frankly, dour. And yet I like it a lot. I went there often when the boys were small, to walk by the river, pick blackberries or paddle in the shallows.

We returned today for the first time in years, walking from Cilrhedyn to Llanychaer, the same route as always. It's not the most beautiful of paths, at least not by Pembrokeshire standards, and yet it has a rustic charm. The farms are worked hard, there are dead ploughs in the fields, an abandoned tractor by the bridge; the woods are left alone.

It seems the people of the Gwaun like doing things their own way. The valley is known for celebrating *Hen Galan*, an alternative New Year based on the Julian calendar – equivalent to our 13th of January. On that day, or many others for that matter, the pubs pay scant regard to licensing laws. As if to confirm this quirkiness, one of its better-known farms is Penlan Uchaf, which promotes the unlikely combination of beef from Longhorn cattle and a show garden for visitors. And at Llanychaer there's another farm that incorporates a flush loo, an iron sculpture of a rat catcher (*or perhaps it's a miner*) and a kitchen range built into the wall!

But for me, the Gwaun is all about the river. The valley sides are steep, making for fast run off after rain, tributaries swell the flow. Today it was dashing over gravel and churning through the falls. Trees on either bank grow down to the water's edge and our path crossed many rills running between their roots. Outside of summer, it's not a walk for keeping feet dry.

In winter, the river turns quickly to spate. I've kayaked it many times, and though never too hard it keeps coming at you. Below Llanychaer the river has carved a gorge, the walls colonised by rhododendrons. There's no way out, other than the flow, and though it is only a few miles to the sea the water can't wait; rapids follow in quick succession, no eddies, no place to stop – until, more swiftly than you expect, the last rush over cobbles into Fishguard harbour.

It's somehow satisfying to finish a journey at the sea. I have kayaked all over the world, made descents of major rivers in Asia and the Alps, but I can think of none with a more delightful finale than the Gwaun. The harbour is one of the most picturesque in Wales; in the Sixties it was used as the film set for Under Milk Wood. And yet there is no attempt to cash in, no shops, no pubs, no commemorative plaques.

Some might say that's an opportunity missed. To me, it's typical of this river, and one of the reasons I like it so much.

Playing With Words

A friend of mine wrote recently on his blog of the delights of 'playing' in the Brechfa Forest. Always alert to the use of language, I'm aware he's echoing a trend amongst outdoor enthusiasts to refer to their exploits as 'play'. I have used the phrase myself: *playing in the rapids* is commonplace jargon of kayakers.

But their use of the word is more loaded. By describing extreme mountain biking – or surfing, climbing and snowboarding *et al* – as 'playing', they're seeking to emphasise a carefree aspect of these activities. They're giving a not so subtle two fingers to the rules and regulations and health and safety junk that stifle the outdoor experience.

They're saying something about themselves too. *Hey, I'm cool enough to use a word like 'play'; I'm in touch with my sensitive side...* And in many cases they position play as a contrast to work; not rejecting the latter, but suggesting it isn't the 'be all' of life. Some go further and disingenuously hint that play is all that matters.

This wordplay strokes their ego. For we know that activities like riding a black run or kayaking white water are fraught with danger. Being on the edge, that fine line between control and wipe-out, isn't play in the normal sense of the word. Only those with the requisite skill and courage can take part – by calling this play, they are making a statement as surely as a peacock displaying its feathers.

I can forgive this, for their intentions are honourable enough – and I have sympathy for their message. We need a better balance in our lives; we need to find meaning beyond work, and the outdoors is one way to that end. At times, we just need some fun.

But herein lies a slight danger. It is hubris to see the landscape as our playground. The Brechfa forest is more than its mountain bike trails – and though I know my friend would feel this way too, not everyone does. Visit the French Alps in the summer, see the pistes and high rise apartments that the winter visitors never view without snow, and think again if playing is without a dark side.

There is a need for balance here. The landscape should be enjoyed; there's nothing wrong with playing in it (if you're inclined to use the phrase) but we should not seek to reduce it to our level. For it is bigger than we are, beyond our control and out of our bounds; ultimately, unknowable.

For The Love Of It

'We'll have to climb this height again,' I panted.

We were cycling out of Morzine, before the sun had risen over the peaks. Mist hung in the valley, cooling us as we climbed the first hill of the day. In the distance, Mont Blanc was emerging from a veil of cloud.

I put my hand on your back as I rode to your side. 'We've gone wrong Mike,' I said, 'this road takes us back to where we started.'

You were sitting upright, your hands off the bars, rooting in the pockets at the back of your jersey. I struggled to keep pace.

And I remember, as you pulled ahead, how you turned and smiled over your shoulder before replying.

'So?'

So?

One syllable, and yet the moment you said it I knew something between us had changed.

You weren't being rude, though sometimes your confidence appears that way. You simply said what you felt. *So we'll have to climb this height again; so what?*

As I crested the hill I watched your blue jersey streak ahead, freewheeling the hairpins, back to Morzine.

We'd been in France for a fortnight but hadn't cycled as much as I'd hoped. It was our last day and I'd persuaded you to try climbing the Col de Joux Plane. I say persuaded because I thought you'd be anxious at riding such a big mountain, not because you wouldn't want to try.

You knew the Col well enough. The summer before we'd stood there, cheering at the riders in the Dauphiné Libéré. You'd wanted to see Lance Armstrong in one of his last races, so we'd driven up at dawn and waited all morning, your brother kicking at patches of snow to kill the time.

It wasn't the first time you'd insisted on seeing a cycle race. When you were eight years old you'd stood for five hours at the roadside barriers, refusing to move as you waited for the Tour de France; the riders flashed by in seconds.

I caught you on the descent, as the road spiralled into Morzine. It was getting narrower, twisting between the chalets, their verandas bleached silver by the sun. A dog snapped at our heels as we rode under lines of washing. You sprinted ahead, into the shower a field sprinkler that was casting beyond the vegetable gardens.

When you were younger I'd thought your brother Daniel would be the cyclist. He could ride a skateboard better than you; he could surf and swim and paddle a canoe better than you. Whenever you competed, whatever the game, I just assumed you'd come in second. He had such natural balance.

So it was Daniel I'd cajoled and held upright as he learned to ride his bike, while you watched from the side. I remember you complaining that holding him was 'cheating'. It was Daniel I took to the cycle club, and it was Daniel who I told your Mum to watch on the evening they held races for the children. Look out for Daniel I said; see how well he rides.

You rode that evening too, but only after you'd nagged and nagged me to let you come. Your bike still had stabilisers; I'd never thought to take them off. I removed them the day before the races, and I remember how I ran by your side, waiting for you to fall.

But even then you rode away, round the green – beyond my reach.

*

The sun still hadn't reached the lower slopes, though the shadows were creeping up the valley. A plane inched its way between the peaks, drawing a thin trail through the palest of blue skies.

As we rode out of Morzine, this time on the correct route, we could see what lay ahead: the road climbed by the side of a gorge, rising in a series of vicious hairpins before reaching a terrace of meadows.

We rode in silence. All the while the gradient steepened.

'Try and keep going; it flattens out after this.'

You smiled, unconvinced.

'You'll be fine. Just watch how I do it.'

As the road passed a waterfall, I stood out of the saddle, using my weight to force the pedals. 'It's easier if you stand up,' I said.

You stayed sitting, your legs spinning with minimal effort, quickly pulling away. As you approached the first hairpin I watched you rise from your saddle, dance on the pedals, and cruise through the bend in a fluid, effortless, arc. You rode each one the same: a synergy of power and leg speed that most cyclists train for years to achieve.

'Well done...' I gasped. I hadn't the breath for more.

You waited for me at the top of the rise.

'How far now?' you asked, grinning.

'About eight kilometers.' I gulped the water from my bottle.

'Does it get any steeper?'

'Not for a while.' I wiped the sweat from my eyes and pointed out the way. 'We climb through the meadows into those woods.' The fir trees hugged the side of the mountain; shafts of sunlight filtered over the summit. 'After the trees it's more hairpins to the top. You'll need to take it steady.'

You started off without me.

'I'll try and keep up,' I called.

Daniel soon said he'd had enough of bikes and didn't want to ride any more, I thought he was just upset; he hadn't won the cycle club race; perhaps the rain had put him off? The results showed you'd ridden faster than anyone your age by a huge margin, but it still didn't register with me.

So I bought Daniel a new bike – he rode it twice then said he hated all the gears. You used to look at it in the garage, measuring yourself against the height of the crossbar. And when I brought home a tiny racing bike I'd found in a dusty second-hand shop, you pinched yourself to check you weren't dreaming. It reminded me of my own first bike, and you loved it just the same.

Do you remember that winter, how you used to ride with me on Sundays? I'd tell you to wear extra layers and bring gloves; always I'd end up giving you mine because you'd forget. Once, miles from home, I took off my socks for you to wear over your hands. Mostly we rode the first half of the club's Sunday outing, your mum collecting us from a café somewhere along the route. Gradually we increased the miles; gradually you became stronger. By summer you were seven years old and Daniel had given you his bike with all the gears. You wanted to go further, faster.

I remember the Easter you rode your first proper race. I have a photo of it by my desk. You're the youngest on the starting line, next to children who are experienced racers, sporting the colours of their clubs; you're wearing a baggy tee-shirt because we couldn't buy a small enough jersey. 'Just have fun,' I told you, 'don't worry about the others.' You finished second, yards behind a boy who'd been racing for years.

Driving home I asked if you'd enjoyed it.

'I'm pleased,' you said. 'But I'm never coming second again.'

And you were right – you didn't lose again that year.

We rode steadily through the meadows, passing rows of beehives and occasional summer chalets. As we stopped to fill our bottles from a stream I pointed to a speck in the distance that was our hotel. Across the valley the cable cars were taking passengers to summits beneath the height we'd reached; you noticed some of the gondolas had mountain bikes slung on their side.

'Lots of people use the cable cars to bring bikes up the mountains,' I explained. 'Then they ride down for fun.'

'It's not fair,' you said. 'They should cycle up like us.'

Always you were so obsessed with fairness. I reasoned it came from being a younger sibling; or perhaps it was your competitive instinct. But I think, even then you were aware of what it means to achieve something entirely through your own efforts. I'd noticed how increasingly you'd wanted to win races with your own tactics and in your own style. We used to argue about whether you should ride away or wait for the final sprint. You still wanted my support, but on your own terms.

As we rode past a chalet surrounded by spruce trees, you said, 'When I become a professional cyclist...'

'A professional, eh?' I jibed.

'Yes,' you replied coolly. 'When I'm a professional, I'm going to buy you a chalet like that.'

'Why's that?'

'So you can watch me whenever I race.'

I was smiling as we came out of the woods, into the glare of the alpine sun.

*

After a year of racing you began to cycle more seriously. We'd ride after school; every weekend we'd be off to an event; if it rained we'd go to the velodrome. And if we weren't riding together we were talking about bikes, plotting victories, planning trips, sharing jokes.

Did I love you more because you cycled so well?

Probably I did, but it wasn't just that. I loved the closeness we developed, the hours in the car travelling together, the shared interests and the private world we'd created. I was your father and your mentor, but increasingly, despite your age, you were taking part on equal terms. That summer you rode your first alpine pass; you were cheered to the summit by a group of astonished onlookers. They lifted you from your bike, rubbing your legs and exclaiming, '*Il est un professional, oui?*' You were eight years old.

I remember being so proud. In a sense, it wasn't you they were cheering, it was me. And later, it wasn't just you who won those races, took all the club trophies and topped the national rankings the following year; it was me too. You were the beautiful, talented, astonishing bike rider that I'd always wanted to be. I loved you so much for it, that at times I lost sight of anything and everybody else.

Limestone cliffs towered above us as we rode towards the final hairpins. My hands were numb from gripping the bars, sweat stung my eyes; I could barely focus beyond my front wheel.

'Look at the names painted on the road,' you called. 'Are they from the Tour de France?'

'I think so.' I was rocking the bike, searching for leverage, each revolution harder than the last. The tarmac was pitted and cracked; streams of water ran down the camber of the bends carrying silt and grit from the cliffs above. 'Watch out for this gravel when we come down – it's very *dangerous*.'

'I'll be fine,' you said, pulling a yard or two ahead.

'And don't drift wide on the bends.'

'Is that Mont Blanc?' you said, pointing to the horizon and ignoring my warning.

'Listen to me Mike. What did I just tell you?'

'I know how to descend Dad.'

'You don't know everything' I snapped. I was tired and irritated. I had thought you would need my help; that my experience would still count for something. Instead, the climb had confirmed how much things had changed; how far you had left me behind.

But there was more to it than that: the descent wasn't especially *dangerous* but you knew why I was worried, you knew what I feared.

'I'm not going to fall, Dad.'

'Just be extra careful.'

'You don't need to keep telling me.'

You rode ahead, leaving me alone. Though I knew you couldn't hear me, I shouted anyway.

'Just one slip Mike. That's all it takes… just one slip'

'Just one slip.'

As you rode away my mind returned to an evening three months earlier.

It was supposed to have been fun – something different – a blast round the BMX track – not even proper cycling. And it was all going so well, until someone said…

'Is that your lad who's fallen off?'

'That'll teach him to ride a BMX,' I joked and we waited for you to pick yourself up from the dirt; nothing damaged save for a little of your pride.

Except you didn't move – and there was a frozen moment as the laughter subsided before the medics rushed over and I realised something was wrong.

Suddenly I was tearing across the track, pulling at your face helmet, the visor streaked red, your shirt covered in blood and you gasping for breath.

And when the helmet finally came off I wiped your mouth and you coughed between broken teeth as I checked for cuts on your tongue – found none – and wondered why there was so much blood. For a moment you smiled and I was reassured, except I was still asking myself where the blood was coming from… desperate to stop it… where the fuck was it coming from?

Then I saw it: the slow sickening trickle that flowed from your ear and wouldn't stop, no matter how many times I wiped it away.

Later in the emergency ward after they x-rayed your skull I noticed the red sticker the nurse placed on your report card.

'What's that for?' I asked.

'It means there's a problem.'

The doctor forbade me to follow as they rushed you for a head scan and I phoned home but was violently sick as I told Mum what had happened. As I waited for her to arrive I found myself trying to pray. But the more I tried, the more I realised it left me hollow. It wasn't so much that I didn't believe, it's because there were no words or promises that could assuage the enormity of my fears. I didn't want to put my trust in anyone, let alone God; I wanted for us change places. I wanted it to be my blood that was flowing onto the pillow.

They wheeled you back and I watched you lying on the bed. You were asleep, a crimson halo around your head and the trickle still refusing to stop.

The nurse brought me some tea, which I couldn't drink; she said doctors would speak to me later.

I phoned home again, but Mum was already on her way.

I had never felt so alone.

We didn't stay long at the top. I bought you a Coke from the cafe and we watched some riders climbing from the south side. A family arrived by car and unhitched their mountain bikes from a roof rack, preparing to descend to Morzine.

'We should have done that,' I joked.

'It's cheating,' you said a little too loudly. The car had a British number plate and the family glared at as both; I shrugged an apology.

We set off soon after, the British family riding a few minutes ahead of us. As we rounded the first corner you tucked your head over the bars, hands poised on the brake hoods and called to me, 'I'm going to catch them.'

'Stay with me, Mike,' I pleaded. 'Let's go down together.'

But you stamped on your pedals and dropped into the shadow of the mountain.

'You must have been going very fast,' the doctor explained as he showed you the x-ray. The fall from the BMX had broken your jaw and the speed of the impact had driven the fracture into your ear.

It was a week since the accident and you couldn't move your mouth to smile.

He said you'd been lucky: the break had aligned itself and your eardrum wasn't badly damaged; a month of jelly and ice cream and you'd be fine.

'Can I ride my bike?' was all you mumbled in reply.

'You're quite something aren't you' he'd said. 'I guess so – but not for a few weeks.'

I was less happy about the prospect.

'You can't wrap me up,' you'd complain, 'it was just a silly accident.'

Within two weeks you were riding again.

By the time we came to the Alps, it was a distant hiccup to you. I was the one who had the nightmares.

You were away from me in yards.

'Be careful,' I called. 'Watch for the grit.'

I tried to keep pace but my back wheel skidded on the first tight bend. You were already well below me – I knew following was pointless.

So I stopped and watched you descending, your body leaning side to side, a touch or two on the brakes, as you rode effortlessly down the mountain. Logically, I knew you'd be fine. But as your blue jersey faded from sight I was overwhelmed with a sense of loss. I found myself mouthing my thoughts,

Not yet, Mike; not just yet…

I got back on my bike and chased as fast as I dared.

You were waiting by a water trough, near the old chalets that stand by the meadows on the rise we'd stopped at earlier. Storms were gathering over Lac Léman as they do most afternoons, Mont Blanc was shrouded in clouds.

'I caught those cheating mountain bikers,' you said. 'They went off on one of the easy trails.'

'I thought you'd left me for good – I was worried, Mike.'

You looked across the valley to avoid my eyes. 'Sorry. I wanted to see how fast I could go.'

'And did you find out?'

You smiled but didn't say.

'We ought to get back.' I moved aside so you could take the lead. 'Mum and Daniel will be waiting.' I explained.

'We can ride together, if you like.'

'Yes,' I said. 'I'd like that very much.'

I Have Always Loved Bikes

I have always loved bikes.

My mother bought my first from the bin-men; I'd spotted it hanging from the back of their cart as they passed our house. She paid them ten shillings and made me share it with my brother. It was purple and red with a step-through frame and a white sprung saddle. I learned to ride with stabilisers, removing one, then the other a few weeks later. When I first rode without them, I pedalled straight into the back of a parked car, knocking myself out.

That bike gave me my first taste of freedom. I'd cycle down our tree lined road, turning right into Etal Avenue, then left to the cul-de-sac by the station, where I'd watch the children on the other side of the line, laughing as they sledged down the railway sidings on wooden boards.

Later I was given a green Hercules that had been standing for years. I spent weeks taking it apart, scraping the rust with brillo-pads, polishing the chrome. It had a three-speed Sturmey-Archer hub, but only two gears ever worked. Not that it mattered; to my eyes it had a cross bar, thin wheels and, most important of all, drop handlebars. It was a racer!

I soon learned that my Hercules was no racer at all, and that Sturmey-Archer gears were the stuff of derision amongst the cognoscenti at school. Ten speed derailleurs were the right stuff; Raleigh Choppers were acceptable too – they were best for giving 'backies' and were popular with the kids from the railway estate.

You'd find it hard to buy a junior racing bike nowadays, though the Chopper is making a comeback, re-launched as a retro alternative to the mountain bike. My boys don't see the appeal. 'It's like a girls' bike,' they say.

'One wheel's smaller than the other.' I think it's marketed at dads – like those who, years ago, longed to ride on the other side of the tracks.

The F Word

Jane was making lunch as I came into the kitchen.

'What are we having?' I asked.

'Just ham and pickles.'

'That'll be nice, won't it,' I said to Dylan, who was at home because of a Teacher Development day.

'I don't know,' he sighed, 'It's all fuck fucky fuck!'

There was moment's silence as I considered this reply. Jane, who is less philosophic about these things, dropped the pickles immediately. 'Who told you THAT word? It's a VERY bad word.' You can imagine what followed.

Evidently he'd heard it at school – or so he said. Someone taught him, but he wasn't sure who. Jane left him in no doubt that regardless of where he'd heard it, if he wanted tea, TV or indeed any sort of niceness he'd better not use THAT word again. 'He's been at school a month,' she moaned, 'and look what happens. At least Daniel and Mike took a year!'

I tried a little diplomacy. After all he has no idea what the word means – and to be honest his Dad's pretty free with the odd 'fuck it' and worse when things go wrong. 'We're having none of your clever stuff, over this,' said Jane. 'If his teachers hear him speak like that, he'll be in big trouble. And in any case it's rude and uncouth.' I've learned when it's best not to argue.

All was soon smoothed over, the incident put down to a one-off. Until early on Saturday morning, when his brother was winding him up, Dylan shouted from his bedroom, 'Stop being a fucker, Mike.' I turned over and looked at Jane.

Five minutes later Dylan was in no doubt about the consequences of the F word and it's multi-variants. There would be no beach today, and no ice cream – there was talk of soap and the washing of mouths. I stayed out of it, suppressing a smile at the accuracy of his comment. After all, Mike was being a nasty... brother. I doubt we will hear the F word again though, at least not for a while.

Some parents get very wound up over swearing. I've seen mothers demanding to see the teacher, speak to the Head, squaring up to mums in the playground – on one occasion swearing so liberally it was fairly obvious where the *bad influence* might have come from. I'm more relaxed; it's a phase kids go through and usually a few tellings off will sort it. If they knew what they were saying it might be different, but frankly, Dylan could just as easily have said 'Tickety boo big boobies'.

Jane wouldn't like that either. And neither would I, for though I might be more sanguine than she is about the F word, I basically agree: it's uncouth, and somehow particularly so in children. Jane never swears and we neither of us would in everyday speech. If I occasionally let fly, it's through anger or a stubbed toe, but then everyone curses when they stub a toe, don't they?

Jane thinks the subtleties of language are best left to adults; as far as Dylan is concerned it's a case of *do as I say, not as Dad does*. Which he's generally taken to heart – certainly he was repentant today. And in the afternoon, as we gathered for some tea, he sat in his chair uncommonly silent – before letting off a long, and I have to say melodious, fart!

Butterflies

About once a decade, there is mass migration of butterflies to the UK. Lepidopterists used to call these *edusa* years, after the former Latin name for the Clouded Yellow, one of the more notable visitors. The phenomenon is a sort of entomological El Nino, predicable in the broadest sense, yet mysterious in its cause and uncertain in its outcome.

In truth, the butterflies migrate here every year. Red Admirals, quintessential to the English country garden, arrive each spring from North Africa. So too do rarities such as the Queen of Spain Fritillary, the Monarch and the Camberwell Beauty.

But *edusa* years are special.

Over a single weekend, millions of butterflies cross from France; newspapers carry articles about a winged invasion, and allotment gardeners (unnecessarily) stock up on protective netting. *Summer's come early*, people say, *Let's hope it lasts.*

For the entomologist the migrations are special for other reasons. One Victorian collector devoted his entire summer to capturing Clouded Yellows. Today, the motivations are different. The abundance of the arrivals allows us to observe migration patterns that are seldom seen. But there is concern too, for the unstoppable tide can threaten resident species, which struggle to recover when the visitors have gone.

Last year, on the evening of Whit Sunday, I went to camp at St David's Head. My teenage son, Daniel, came with me. He had had a row with his mother over staying out late and chose camping as preferable to being grounded at home.

The Head, as we call it, is ten miles from my house; its miniature mountain, Carn Llidi, dominates the horizon. I have been there hundreds of times: walking the path from Whitesands, running the cliffs from Abereiddy, shortcutting to Porth Melgan through the hidden valley where the feral ponies graze. I have kayaked there too; even swum against the rip, seals grunting as I climbed the black walls to the wave-washed platform where the land and sea collide.

Officially, it is forbidden to camp on the Head. But if you pitch late and pack up early nobody seems to mind. We took the route from Whitesands, stopping at Porth Melgan to fill our bottles from the smugglers' brook. It was muggy, the tide at slack, the sea a deep indigo; shearwaters glided low over the bay, returning to their burrows on Skomer.

'I think I'll sleep in the bivvy,' Daniel said.

'It'll be cold; there's a clear sky.'

'I like the stars,' he replied, grinning. 'And no offence Dad, but you snore.'

Daniel was fourteen that year, feeling his way into manhood, bristling for freedom and clashing often with his mother. He tested me with humour or sulking more than outright defiance. As we neared the Head it was he who noticed the birds.

'Look Dad, what's happening by the rocks?'

Fifty yards off shore there is a granite platform. Hundreds of swallows and martins were crisscrossing the air above it. There were birds on the Head too; wheatears, and warblers, probably others, though I couldn't tell. By the time we reached the cromlech, the swallows had had moved nearer the land. A kestrel swooped into the melee, the other birds unconcerned by its presence.

We sat on the boulders at the summit, the horizon nearing the sun, the sky now crimson. Bats began arriving; dozens of them, freaking around us in that tumbling flight that makes me want to cover my head.

'They're catching moths,' said Daniel, 'they're coming from Ramsey.'

A column of insects began to pass us, their wings silhouetting against the sun. I started to count them: twenty, thirty, fifty... it was hopeless; there were thousands, gathering on the warm rocks as the birds feasted in the last of the light.

'I suppose you knew the moths were coming,' Daniel added, 'that's why we came here wasn't it?'

'I had no idea,' I replied. 'And they're not moths; they're Painted Ladies.'

I know precisely when I saw my first Painted Lady: the nineteenth of August 1972, in my Aunt Marjorie's garden on my eleventh birthday.

Marjorie wasn't my real aunt. She was our primary school nurse and a friend of my mother. Her husband had died in India, he'd worked with Lord Hunt who'd led the first ascent of Everest. She drove a red Ford Capri, seldom bothering with the gears; her house was stuffed with Indian artefacts and Catholic icons.

Looking back, I realise it was a place of escape for my mother. At the depths of my father's depression she would take me there from school. I'd be sent to the garden, Marjorie explaining they had 'things to talk about.' And she would give me a jar and tell me to hunt for caterpillars. 'Try not to get lost,' she'd joke, 'it's a wilderness out there.'

And she wasn't exaggerating. Her garden ran down to the railway, the lawn a meadow; the borders overgrown with foxgloves, convolvulus, and climbing nasturtiums.

There were patches of stinging nettles and thistles, forgotten beds of sedum and torch lilies that we called 'red hot pokers'. Backing onto the line were three buddleias, each large enough for a small boy to hide in: two bloomed a Prussian Blue (still my favourite colour), the other a pure white.

We stopped calling at Marjorie's the year I left for Grammar School; the same year my mother learned to drive and found other freedoms. I was older too and had more exciting things to do than visit my mother's elderly friend.

But sometimes, in the summer especially, I would cycle there and pretend to be passing. We'd head down the garden to look at the buddleia. She kept records in a notebook and I remember her being quite excited about the Painted Lady. 'They come from India,' she said. 'My husband said they were pilgrims. How nice that one should come on your birthday.'

'Why do you like butterflies so much?' Daniel asked.

'I like most things about nature.'

'Yes, but everyone knows you like butterflies best,' he sighed.

'I used to watch them in my aunt's garden. She taught me their names.'

'Was that the aunt who came to visit; the mad one?'

'You mean eccentric.'

'You know what I mean, Dad.'

Marjorie had come when the boys were small. Though almost blind, she'd travelled four hundred miles by train. We'd sat in the garden, the children bouncing on their trampoline. I've always wanted to go on one of those, she'd cried. Downing a sherry, she'd tucked her dress in her knickers and climbed up. For years the boys referred to her as Auntie Bloomers.

'When I was about your age, I made a net to see what else I could find. Blues and Skippers and such like.'

'Blues and Skippers.' Daniel mimicked my voice. 'You're the only person in Wales who'd say that.'

'Don't worry Dan, there's no one around to hear.'

I unpacked the tent on a circle of turf. As I lay it out, a flurry of butterflies rose from the ground. It was almost dark, the birds had left though the Painted Ladies were still arriving. The bats continued their lunatic flapping by the cliff.

Daniel watched me struggling with the tent.

'Didn't your dad mind?' he asked. 'Didn't he think butterflies were a bit... you know?'

'Sissy?'

'I suppose.'

'It kept me out the house. Other than that he didn't much care.'

'I wish Mum was like that.'

'No you don't,' I snapped. 'The only interest my Dad showed was giving me fifty quid after winning on the horses. He said to buy any daft thing I wanted'

Daniel jumped down from the rocks to help me.

"What did you get?'

'A moth trap,'

'You were so cool,' he sniggered. 'I suppose you just went to the local butterfly shop to get it?'

I unrolled the sleeping mat.

'If you must know, I caught the train to London, slept overnight at Kings Cross and came back the next day.'

'Oh. So how old were you?'

'Fourteen.'

Marjorie was wrong about the Painted Ladies; they come from Morocco not India. Somewhere in the Atlas Mountains are vast breeding grounds, though the exact locations are unknown. In *edusa* years, these presumably become overcrowded and the adults are forced to travel north.

The adult butterflies, the *imagos*, breed along the migration corridors; in a hot summer they manage two or even three broods. The caterpillars or *larvae* can thrive on mallow or hawthorn, but their preferred food-plant is thistle, in which they spin protective nets before *pupating* on the stems.

I prefer the word chrysalis to *pupa*. It comes from the Greek for golden and refers to the iridescent sheen on the outer skin. The Painted Lady chrysalis is aggressively thorny, designed to be hidden in undergrowth – yet each ridge has a jewel-like spike that dazzles in the sunlight.

Despite the numbers that arrive, resident colonies have not established in the UK. Those adults that stay will die in the frost; very few return south.

I woke early.

A gull watched me as I walked to the edge; a Cormorant on the rocks below was holding its wings aloft.

Daniel lay foetal in his bivvy-bag, the drawstring tight to his face. The contents of his sack were strewn across the turf, the bag itself a makeshift pillow. I found the stove amongst the mess and lit it, shielding the match until the flame hissed under the kettle.

The Painted Ladies were still arriving. There were two on Daniel's bag, more on the tent and one on the rock beside me. It probed the lichen for moisture, unfolding its proboscis and flashing its chequered wings, the black edges like mascara. For an insect that had travelled so far it looked remarkably fresh.

The kettle rattled.

'We need to be off.' I nudged Daniel and offered him some coffee.

'Don't want any,' he grunted.

I packed the tent and waited for him to wake. He began shuffling from item to item, filling his rucksack without getting out of the bivvy-bag. When everything else was packed he slipped out and forced it, dripping, into the neck of the sack.

'Interesting technique,' I quipped.

'We're going home aren't we?'

'And you'll be walking all the way, if you don't watch that tone.'

'Sorry.' He shouldered his sack and waited for me to rise.

The sun lifted the mist as we walked to the car, a couple of surfers were drifting offshore, hoping for the swell to pick up. Daniel stayed close; I sensed he wanted to talk.

'What happens to the butterflies?' he asked.

'A few will stay here. Most keep travelling north.'

'So will you try and capture one? Like in France, when you caught that Purple Emperor?'

'Don't tell me you want to go on a butterfly hunt?'

'No chance,' he laughed. But later he said, 'You should take Dylan to catch butterflies; he'd like it and you'd have a good time.' Dylan was five at the time.

The path narrowed but Daniel stayed by my side, his pack brushing me.

'You know what you said about going to London?'

I slowed, and so did he.

'Do you think that maybe I could …'

'Not London,' I said. 'But yes, maybe.'

He smiled as our eyes met, skipping ahead of me.

'So when do you think…'

'I'll talk to your Mum,' I said. 'Now get a move on, she promised to have breakfast ready.'

*

It was a good summer for butterflies; my notebook lists twenty-three species, fifteen of them from the garden. I recorded my first Green Hairstreak and discovered a colony of Grayling on the rocks at Cleg Yr Boia.

I didn't camp again with Daniel last year. He wanted to be with his friends; off to town, staying out late; sometime just to be alone. Did we mind if he stayed at home, he asked, when we suggested a weekend away?

'He's not old enough,' Jane argued.

'We're only going overnight.'

''That's not the point,' she tried to sound firm.

'But you let him go to Cardiff,' I countered. 'And he slept over at the festival.'

'That was different.'

'No it isn't – except this time he's in his own house.'

'It just feels… a bigger step.'

We left him with a fridge full of food and a list of instructions: sausages for lunch, text us twice a day, stay overnight at Grandma's, and if you've any problems, phone our hotel.

By the autumn, if we went away we assumed he wouldn't be coming. Dylan had become my new camping buddy. 'Can we sleep at the beach,' he would ask, or sometimes simply 'let's camp in the garden Dad!' I took him further afield, but not much.

And Daniel encouraged him. He bought him a torch and gifted him his sleeping bag. Camping's cool he'd tell him – especially with your big Dad! And if he put him to bed, he'd tell him stories of France and Austria and where he'd camped when he was five.

There was a brief Indian Summer as the sedum came into flower. I'd planted it in the shelter of a wall that reflects the afternoon sun. The last of the Painted Ladies would come to feed, along with Commas and Admirals and a Hummingbird Hawk Moth that next door's cat grabbed as I watched, helpless, from the shed.

There was still the occasional butterfly coming when my mother phoned.

'Marjorie died last week,' she said at the end of her call. 'She was the nurse at your school, do you remember?'

Ninety-five and sharp a as knife, they said at the funeral. She'd have gone on longer, except her son had died that summer.

But she'd given up after that; couldn't last the winter.

There was no *edusa* this year. But a good spring brought Orange Tips in numbers and the Tortoiseshells survived the snow; the Grayling colony has thrived and I've seen many at the Head this summer. Dylan comes with me on my recording trips though he'd rather I liked trains. We've seen twelve Painted Ladies.

Daniel has a girlfriend. She seems to live at our house, if not physically, then on Facebook. In a year they've spent more time together than most people do in five. She's a frail little thing with long auburn hair and wide eyes and dark mascara. I think she's good for him: diligent, determined, a little eccentric. Jane likes her too.

In August I was sorting some books in preparation for house move. In a drawer full of sketchbooks was a copy of The Ascent of Everest, signed by Lord Hunt and given to me by Marjorie that time she came to visit. I'd not looked at it then and had lost it soon after. Inside were lists of butterflies, some from India, the Latin and local names, all carefully dated. Towards the back were her notes from her garden, including an entry I recognised: *Nineteenth of August 1972, Large White, Peacock, Painted Lady.*

I was forty-nine this year; not reason enough for a party. So to celebrate I said I'd take Dylan to camp at the Head.

We were about to leave when Daniel asked if he and his girlfriend could come too.

'If you bring the other tent.'

I could sense Jane calculating the sleeping arrangements, so added loudly and winking at him, 'And you're in the bivvy, Dan.'

'We won't 'do' anything,' he whispered and I clipped him gently round the head.

We walked from Whitesands this time too; camped at the same spot, the shadows lengthening as we pitched the tents. Shearwaters were heading back to Skomer.

'Can I have a story?' Dylan asked'

Daniel sat next to him. 'Once upon a time, there were millions of butterflies...'

'Not more butterflies!' Dylan moaned, and we all laughed.

Why don't you two go for a walk, I said to Daniel.

The moon was above Carn Llidi, a thin crescent in the pale evening light. Dylan sat on my lap, as we watched the two of them scramble to the edge of Wales. They stood, their arms round each other, surrounded by sea but for the crumbling arch that connects the final rocks to the land. Dylan was almost asleep.

'Can we live here,' he asked.

'Just for tonight,' I said.

I hitched him over my shoulder, picking my way between the rocks. As I lay him down to unzip the tent my eye caught a movement in the air – a butterfly. It was chequered and fringed with black, and it flew to where Daniel and his girl were throwing pebbles at the sea.

It was heading south to Ramsey.

You'll Come To Love Both

I remember the first time I came to Abergwesyn. It was the spring of '88 and I was living in Cardiff, questioning my decision to come to Wales after a cold grey winter. I wasn't happy in the city, but didn't feel at home in the hills. South Wales felt alien; even the mountains lacked the stillness I'd come to love in my home of Northumberland. They felt spoiled too, riven by the industrial dereliction that littered the valley floors. I must have mentioned something of the sort in the office.

Roger was having none of it.

'I tell you, Wales is the most beautiful and ugly country in the world,' he said. 'And you'll come to love both.'

Roger lived above Merthyr, a proper Valleys boy, he'd been a coach driver for years, before moving into sales. His chief delight was to visit customers in Carmarthen or Cardigan – *very important they are* – insisting on 'going west' at least once a week.

'You come with me,' he said, 'then decide if you want to stay living in Wales.'

We drove north through Brecon, to Rhayader and over the mountain road to Aberystwyth, stopping for a ten minute chat with a customer, then – work completed for the day – we headed south to Aberaeron. Roger was on a mission: he took me to Lampeter, to Dolaucothi, to the wonderful village of Caio (now one of my favourite places) and then, by yet another double back, to Tregaron and the road to Llanwrtyd. 'Look at this mess,' he complained, as we drove through an area of young forestry, the hillside covered in serried rows of saplings. I murmured agreement, though in truth I was car sick by this point. 'Just you wait,' he said. 'The best valley in Wales is over this hill.'

The pass is a near perfect glacial valley, cut deeper by the Afon Irfon and running from the northern forests of Llyn Brianne to the hamlet of Abergwesyn. We edged down the road that clings like a belvedere to the side of the mountain, stopping at a lay-by above a narrowing of the gorge. 'If you don't like it here,' I remember Roger saying,' you might as well go home.'

I was there again this morning, driving through the stunted oaks at the eastern end of the pass. There was ice on the road, the northern slopes still in shadow by mid morning. On the southern side the bracken was drying in the sun; two ravens harried a buzzard. It's twenty years since Roger first took me here, I have driven and cycled this road dozens of times, and still it takes my breath away.

Abergwesyn Common is owned by the National Trust and consequently it's been saved from the vandalism wrought on the hills beyond. At the head of the pass is a steep road where the forestry begins – appropriately, it's known as the Devil's Staircase. From here to the south and west, swathes of fir trees cloak the hills, the only respite to the monotony being the fell-clearance areas and the Dolgoch hostel, nestling in an oasis of bog that was presumably too awkward to plant. A vast area of land between here and Tregaron has been spoiled – some would say ruined – for what I suspect was little more than politics and the quasi-economics of the forestry commission; but what do I know?

What I do know, is that the fir trees are every bit as ugly and despoiling as the industrial detritus that litters the Rhondda. And this is only one small area of the Mid Wales forests. Huge areas of the Cambrian Mountains have suffered the same fate, and sadly I suspect it will be repeated – though today it is wind farms more than trees that the politicians desire.

And yet I still love this area. Today, I walked to the bothy at Moel Prysgau. It is miles from any tarmac, approached by the old drove road to Strata Florida. The path hugs the river, sometimes this side, sometimes that – time and again you have to wade and flounder through the peat to stay with it. A few miles in and the paths become forest roads, complete with junctions and rights of way, the views more sporadic. In a sense it is the reverse of walking in the South Wales Valleys – the dereliction, in the form of inappropriate planting, is above you, not below. Yet there's a remoteness here, a stillness that saves the landscape despite our worst efforts. And if you climb high enough, to the north at least, you can eventually crest the trees.

Towards the end of my walk I came to a boggy pool near the summit of Drygarn Fach, two geese floated on the surface, untroubled by my watching. From here I looked over the Common, down on the river Irfon, the gorge and its oaks, across the swathe of forestry that runs to the southern side of Llyn Brianne. And I remembered what Roger had said – about Wales being the most beautiful and ugly country – and I thought how right he was.

He was right about me too: for I have come to love both.

True Geordies Cry

As I drove the last few miles into Newcastle I saw the Angel of The North. The sheer size of the sculpture stirred me from darker thoughts. Its colossal wings seemed to be reaching out – a gesture of welcome for a prodigal son. Except, as I passed underneath, I realised it was almost symmetrical; what I'd taken as a welcome, could just as easily have been the angel turning its back.

In Wales, where I live now and where I'd driven from that morning, to describe a longing for home they use the word *hiraeth*. I had wondered if I'd feel something of the sort. But as I crossed the Tyne Bridge and looked down on the new quayside, I could only think that I'd made good time and with a little luck, might miss the rush hour traffic.

I was parking the car when there was a rap on the windscreen. An old man was mouthing something to me through the glass. He was pitifully thin.

I lowered the window a couple of inches.

'You can't park here son. You're blocking the drive.' He pointed to the house opposite with one of his sticks, holding the roof of my car for balance. His shirt billowed in the breeze.

I put the car into reverse but he gripped the lip of the window, peering at me though the glass. His face was wrinkled, white hairs bunching in his nose and ears. 'Back up son,' he said, 'you'll be fine down the road.'

There was a familiar lilt to his voice and I realised, with something akin to horror, that he was using the word 'son' literally.

It was the first time I'd seen my father in twenty years.

He released his grip and I backed the car down the road.

When I turned to face him again, he was shuffling towards the house.

I sat with my hands on the steering wheel watching him cross the road. Some boys were playing football, using the gap between a lamppost and a car as a makeshift goal. A teenage girl who was pushing a flimsy buggy had stopped to watch them. One of the boys scored and the ball ran towards my father but they waited for him to pass before retrieving it.

I reached for my briefcase, taking out a large envelope. Inside it were dozens photographs that Jane had given me to show him. They would be something to talk about she'd said.

I chose three, leaving the rest on the seat.

My father left me waiting by the door.

He was talking to some workmen who were fixing the guttering on his neighbour's house. He was saying something about a camera that was fixed to the wall. Eventually, he turned, offering a cold hand to greet me.

As I entered the house, I glimpsed a silver haired lady in the kitchen. I presumed this was Mary, my father's long time partner – I had phoned her for directions before coming. She waved her hand to indicate I should follow my father into the living room.

The room was bright, more modern than I'd expected: leather sofas, Ercol units, a glass coffee table – there was nothing I recognised. In the corner of the room was a large flat screen TV, a jumble of wires linking it to a lap top computer on a trolley.

My father sat down, adjusted his sticks and pulled the trolley towards him. He started typing on the keyboard.

'I don't expect there's much crime where you live?'

The TV powered up, displaying a black and white shot of the workmen next door. He pressed a key and the screen split into four images, each showing the house from a different angle. I could see the boys playing football; the girl with the pushchair was walking down the street.

'The kids are buggers round here,' he said.

'Once a policeman...' I replied.

He pressed a key and the screen changed to a news channel. There was a bulletin of Gordon Brown making an announcement about the financial crisis. My father waited a moment before speaking.

'The world's gone mad,' he said.

I didn't reply; didn't want to get drawn into conversation. I was shocked by his appearance, still taking in the surroundings. I found myself estimating how much he must weigh; perhaps seven stones. He watched the TV as I scanned the room and waited for him to speak.

'Mary says you're up on business.'

'Yes,' I lied.

'It must be important.'

'Just a meeting.'

'On a Friday afternoon?'

He looked at me and I returned the stare, focusing beyond his eyes so I didn't blink; a technique I'd learned as a child. *Give him detail, don't hesitate...*

'I'm interviewing for an assistant. He's a lawyer from Edinburgh. It was the only time he could make, so we agreed to meet here.'

'Really?'

'Yes,' I replied firmly.

'I'd have thought he'd come to you.'

'For God's sake, Dad.' I shifted in my chair as he looked at me again.

'Did you drive over the new bridge?' he asked. 'They say true Geordies cry when they cross the Tyne.'

'I felt nothing.' My voice was clipped and sharp.

Gordon Brown had finished his announcement, but my father carried on watching, commenting on the bulletins, trying to draw me in. For fifteen minutes he searched for questions, fidgeting in the lull between stories. What did I think would happen to interest rates? Hadn't they made a mess of Iraq? Did I know Kevin Keegan had resigned?

I had forgotten how, before I left the North East, my father would always steer our conversations to current affairs. He didn't do this because he thought I would be interested, though sometimes I allowed the pretence. He did it because it was safe ground. Because by talking about the news he hoped to delay the inevitable. For most times I called, he knew I was coming to confront him.

Nothing has changed I thought – he's still as wary of me as ever.

When I was a child my father had terrified me. He was a big man: muscular, short-tempered and at times, extremely violent. One of my earliest memories is my mother making me a pair of long trousers to hide my bruises in school the next day.

But it wasn't the beatings that terrified me most. It was the ever-present menace, the constant fear they could begin at any moment. And perhaps worst of all, the interrogations that preceded them. My father had an obsession with the truth. If he sensed the tiniest of withholds he would question me again and again, his anger rising until eventually it spilled over into slaps and belts.

As a small child, I had neither the strength nor the words to hit back. My way of coping was to create a world he couldn't be part of. I invented codes to keep secrets from him. I learned his shifts so I could plan my 'escape' when he was out of the house. Once, as a punishment for some misdemeanour, he threw away every one my toys – so I learned to make shadow puppets by shaping my hands; I'd flash the shapes behind his back as an act of defiance.

I was in my early teens before my father was diagnosed with manic depression. Shortly after, he retired from the police on grounds of ill health. Only later did I learn that he'd suffered a breakdown, brought on by years of working in the vice squad. At the height of his illness he would spend days alone in the bedroom, watching the CCTV cameras he had rigged to the eaves. Silence was a given, visitors were banned – even relatives didn't come to our house.

Each of us found our own response. My elder brother withdrew into himself, then left for college. My younger brother – who was spared the worst – became ill with nervous tension. Years later he would suffer from depression and it is perhaps telling that he has remained the closest to and most understanding of my father. My mother invariably turned to me.

Psychologists say that the root cause of anxiety is a dilemma of whether to fight or flee. The adrenaline rush we experience in the face of danger is a primeval response – one that in our 'safe' modern world, we recreate through horror movies, roller-coasters and the like. They say too, that those who seek the biggest thrills – free climbers for instance – are really seeking control; a tiny part of their life where their actions alone determine their fate.

Later in my life I would become a good climber; I would learn too – from my wife and children – that unconditional love brings with it a power to conquer many fears. But at the time there was something else that would give me strength. Something, as it happened, that I learned by accident.

I found that if I stood by the bay window my father wouldn't hit me.

I was perhaps fifteen at the time and I don't recall the reason for the row, but I remember as I backed towards the light he stopped beating me. It was the first time he had ever held back and I realised in an instant why it was happening. I remember the adrenaline too: I began shouting at him, knowing that so long as the neighbours could see me, he wouldn't raise his hand.

Gradually I learned that by facing up to my father I could control him. By the time I was seventeen I was as tall as he was but it wasn't the prospect of my hitting back that stopped him. It was because he knew, no matter how bad his anger, that I would find the strength to confront him.

Often, after one of his outbursts, I would lie awake at night, replaying the scene in my mind, shaking as I recalled his threats and how eventually, he'd backed down.

It was an intoxicating feeling.

A shaft of sunlight flooded the room, making the TV difficult to watch.

'So what else shall we talk about?' he asked.

'Would you like to hear about your grandsons?' I felt for the photographs in my pocket.

'I know all about them,' he said, hauling his thin frame up to the computer. 'This is a marvellous invention for that sort of thing.'

He clicked the mouse and the computer screen displayed my company's website. There was a picture of me and the other directors. 'I always knew you'd do well.'

'And what of my boys?' I asked. 'What do you know about them?'

'I've been following Dylan,' he interrupted. 'He's on the cycling web sites.'

'It's Michael who's the cyclist. Dylan is only three.'

He wasn't flustered by the correction.

'I get confused between them. Hasn't Michael got a Welsh name too?

'His middle name is Huw.'

'That's right, your brother told me.'

'Oh did he?'

'I have a picture of Daniel somewhere,' he said.

He scrolled through photographs on the screen, mainly shots of my younger brother and his family, occasional pictures of my boys. I couldn't tell if he was trying to show me that he cared, as if he were trying to say, *look, I've been following your life from afar.* Or whether it was some sort of defiance – *you thought you'd stop me knowing, but hey, I found out anyway.*

'Who gave you those pictures?'

'I've forgotten – you don't mind do you?'

I curled the photographs Jane had given me in the palm of my hand.

'Should I tell you about Daniel?' I said sharply, raising my voice to make sure he was paying attention. This was my chance to say what I'd come to say.

He turned to face me.

'He's got fair hair and he's six foot tall already: muscular and inquisitive – just like you in lots of ways…'

I looked straight into his sunken eyes, wanting to resurrect the fear I'd carried through childhood, the long buried feelings of contempt. 'Except…'

'Except he's gentle and sensitive – he wouldn't hurt a fly.'

At least, that's what I was going to say. It's what I'd rehearsed on the long drive from Wales.

For over twenty years I'd denied my father any access to my life, cutting off all contact when my job gave me the chance to move away. It was the ultimate control mechanism. I set out to free myself of him, and to do so I'd ensure he knew nothing about me. I told my brothers not to tell him where I lived or to give him any news. He missed my wedding, the births of my sons, my career, and so much more. But I'd reveal it all now; show him how I'd come through. I'd tell him of the three great joys in my life. If the photographs in my hand had been knives I'd have twisted them with pleasure.

Jane had often asked me how I felt about my father. Always I'd answered that I was indifferent. I had cultivated that numbness over the years, coming to realise that indifference is more powerful than hatred or even contempt, both of which demand, at least at some level, that you care.

As my father waited for me to finish the sentence, I realised just how successful I'd been. This wasn't my father; it was a wheezing, fumbling old man who was nervous and threatened by my presence.

The light from the window silhouetted his frail body. I felt no anger, no desire to punish or hurt him any more.

'Except... he's only thirteen,' I said.

My mother finally divorced my father – six months after I left home – but for years he continued to exert his presence on the family. Often he would make threatening phone calls. For a long period he stalked my maternal grandparents. Occasionally he would write rambling letters, threatening suicide and talking of 'taking others with him.'

It never occurred to me not to deal with him, or even to consider involving others. My father was ill – that explained his behaviour if not exactly excusing it – and someone had to make sure he didn't cross the line. It seemed natural that I should take that role. There was also my own rage; a pent up sense of injustice at the way he'd so dominated my life. Looking back, I was spoiling for a fight.

One afternoon, after some incident or other, I went to his house and found him in the street, walking home from the betting shop. I was determined to stop the nonsense once and for all. I warned him that if he continued with his threatening behaviour I'd contact the police and his doctor too. For a moment I thought better of this as for the first time in years he hit me. It was an extraordinary scene. He stripped off his jacket and squared up for a fight, but I stood my ground, daring him to hit me again. I told him he'd made my life hell, that I'd hated him since I was child and that it had to stop. He could punch me all he liked, but he'd never change the past. I was screaming, bawling the words with an anger I'd not felt before.

And as I shouted, far from hitting me again, he sank to his knees and cried. He begged my forgiveness; he loved me really, he said. I remember the neighbours watching from their windows as I turned and left him sobbing him in the road.

That evening, I knew the power had shifted: that he was now as terrified of me, as I had been of him.

Soon after, I moved to Wales.

The news programme had finished.

He was resting in the pile of cushions at the back of his seat, his face tight with pain. The screen had returned to the silent pictures of the house next door; the workmen were packing away their ladders.

Eventually he broke the silence.

'I have a tumour,' he said.

'I know. Mary phoned me last week.'

'They didn't tell me for months, but I knew what it was.'

'Perhaps they weren't certain?'

'They knew; they lied.' he spat the words from between clenched teeth.

I let him go on.

His recalled his visits to the hospital, recounting in detail the dates, the names of the doctors, the tests he endured. They were lying all along, he said. He'd looked up the symptoms on the internet.

'What is the prognosis?'

'You know what they told me?' he snarled, his voice quaking with anger. '*We're talking months, not years.* That's what they said – that and a morphine prescription.'

'What about treatment?'

'They don't give chemotherapy to people my age.' His teeth bit down on his tongue, curling it into the corner of his mouth so it peeped through his lips – a sign we'd feared as children. 'They denied it of course,' he tried to pull himself up but fell backwards at the effort. His face purpled, his teeth ground harder on his tongue.

'They're a bunch of bloody liars,' he sighed, punching the arm of the settee with a soft grey fist.

I have thought a lot about that punch. It was in one way pathetic, and yet at the same time it was somehow noble, a sort of last defiance.

There was nothing more to say.

His face was damp with tears.

A tap on the door interrupted my thoughts and Mary came in with a tray of tea. She put it down and shook my father's arm.

'Are you awake, pet?'

He didn't respond so she covered him in a blanket and sat in the armchair by mine.

'He won't eat,' she whispered, 'but I try to tempt him.'

She passed me a plate of sandwiches that were cut into tiny triangles. 'Forgive me for not saying hello. I thought I'd leave you two together.'

Her face was flushed and she was younger than I'd expected.

My father stirred in his chair and we both watched him, waiting to see if he'd wake.

'It's time for his morphine, but we'll let him sleep shall we?'

I nodded. 'He was showing me his computer,' I said.

'That thing; he's on it all day.'

'It's quite impressive for his age.'

'I suppose it gives him pleasure. He likes searching for information.'

'He was always good at that.'

'Just not so good at other things.' She drank some tea and looked knowingly over the rim of her cup.

'You're aware of the history.'

'I am. But he's changed a lot, you know. We worked on it over the years.'

'Is he still on Valium?'

'Not any more, it's bad for his temper. He gets depressed, but I just say *I'm here if you need me pet*. We've learned to cope together.'

'And what about the anger?'

'It's rare nowadays.' She looked at me sadly. 'He's always sorry after.'

I wanted to say that he always was, but I let it pass.

I'm curiously drawn to this gentle lady and want to ask her what she saw in my father, why she'd stayed with him all these years. And as if anticipating my thoughts she said.

'We've had a quiet life. It's all he could cope with, but he looked after me in his way.'

'Did he ever talk about the past, about when we were children?'

'I tell him he can't change what he's done. Your leaving was a blessing in some ways.'

I placed the photographs on the arm of the chair and reached for my coat.

'This must be Dylan,' she said, pointing to the smallest child in the picture

I leant towards her so we could look at it together.

'And is this one Michael? I hear he's a cyclist.'

We talked about the boys and I explained how they had transformed my life, how becoming a father had been such a revelation – a journey without maps, I said.

She picked up the second photograph.

'This must be Jane – she's very elegant.'

'She'll be pleased when I tell her,' I laughed.

'And is this where you live?' She was looking now at the third photo.

'It's in Pembrokeshire, on the tip of Wales.'

'I went there once,' she replied, 'on a coach trip with your Dad. We went to a castle and I said to him, this is near where Mark lives.'

'You should have called in.'

'I'd have liked that,' she sighed.

Mary showed me to the door.

My father was still asleep; we didn't disturb him.

'You can keep the photographs,' I said. And I kissed her goodbye.

The light was fading when I crossed the Tyne. As I passed the Angel of the North, the last rays of the dying sun slipped below the horizon.

Stanage, Peak District, 2009

It feels odd to be back. I'm not used to the routine: scrabbling for my kit, sheltering under the tailgate as I change into Ron Hills and pull on a thermal. My map flaps in the wind – it's the wrong one – I shove it back in the car. Jane drove this morning, following my directions: *take the road by Ladybower, go up the hill and there's a pull in by a sandy track.* It hadn't changed, nor had the wind, bitter as always. I pull on a hat, stuff my cagoule in the bum bag and set off again.

It's twenty years since I last ran at Stanage. Yet it's all so familiar: the smell of the grit, the friction of the stones, the squelch of peat when I miss my footing. As I run up the hill the sun lifts the mist, by the time I reach Stanage End the sky is pale blue. The edge stretches ahead, I take off my hat and pause – a grouse takes flight from the heather, its red wattles flapping as it crash-lands yards from where I'm standing.

Stanage is the longest of the Derbyshire edges, a five-mile escarpment, running from Bamford to the moors above Hathersage. It's famous for rock climbing, but to me it was always best as a place to run. And as I start to move again, the reasons I felt that way filter back.

It is not so much the landscape, though I like the feel of these open moors, looking down on the greener valleys of the White Peak. It's the process of running here that is a special joy. You have to place your feet carefully, plan your route between the boulders and the mire – skip up rocks, jump from others, dash through the bogs – and you have to do this at speed, for traversing the ground at pace is what gives running its meaning. I'm aware of every step, how it feels to plant and rise; I'm conscious too of the irony that being in such a beautiful place it's the ground underfoot that commands my attention.

The faster I run, the more attuned I become to the path; the decisions come easily, each step flowing into the next. I think of it as a river – I'm scouting the rapids, adjusting my line, at one with the flow. As I reach the main climbing area I've found a natural rhythm, a balance of speed and awareness that for these moments, is all that matters.

The walkers don't acknowledge me; I'm something to be avoided, stood aside from as I pass. It's the climbers who greet me, with nods and waves, a cheer of encouragement. Perhaps they know something of how, though intense concentration, we can transcend our situation – those who've climbed for any period will understand what I'm saying. The last few miles pass without effort.

As I descend to Burbage I spot Jane waiting at the car. The last time I ran this route she was there too. On that occasion I carried on, past Longshaw and Froggatt, Curbar and Birchin, to finish after seventeen miles at the Robin Hood Inn.

But that was twenty years ago, and though returning is one of my chief delights, I know that some things can never come again.

A Turning Tide

On the far tip of Wales, a kilometre south west of St David's Head, lies Ramsey. The stretch of water between it and the mainland offers the hint of safe passage; in reality it is the site of countless shipwrecks. Twice a day the great mass of water which fills St Brides Bay is pulled through Ramsey Sound, creating the largest tide race in Europe. Porpoises have learned to come here, waiting for the fish that are drawn with the tide; this weekend saw a different gathering.

At 4.30 am I'm awoken by rustling downstairs. My friend Debs had come to stay, inviting with her half a dozen others; they're preparing for an early morning trip. These are not average kayakers: Debs, a professional for twelve years, is one of the world's foremost white-water paddlers. Her friends are equally competent, and just as well, for the September equinox brings the biggest tides of the year.

The tide race is known as the Bitches, though the name really belongs to the rocks that funnel the water into narrower channels. As the sea is pulled through the Sound, it is forced over a shelf and further squeezed between pinnacles, creating the standing waves, holes and towbacks which are the reason the kayakers come. At full flow, more than 300,000 cubic meters of water will pass every second – a drifting boat would be a carried at twenty miles an hour over rapids as big as those in the Grand Canyon.

The Bitches has become a popular destination for tourists who venture out on inflatable ribs, powered by water-jet engines. It's a thrilling ride, but it's usually done in the daytime when the tides are smaller and there's safety cover to hand. Paddling out before dawn in a ten foot plastic boat is a different prospect. It is a different experience too.

For in the early morning, as the light slowly fills the sky and the roar of the water subsides into white noise, this is a silent and spiritual place. I was once there when the sea held our reflections like a painting, the horizon of the over-fall melting into an infinite sky. A bull seal watched from the eddy, boils of water turning me in endless circles round his huge dog-like head. All around was elemental chaos, and yet I barely noticed.

In my early thirties I paddled the Bitches hundreds of times. It was the reason I came to Pembrokeshire; I learned to roll a kayak there, I saw my first sunfish; I made life-long friends and eventually bought a house nearby. One time I went out with a friend – we were alone, but nothing could go wrong – except I capsized and on rolling to the surface sliced open my nose, fainting from the rush of blood. My friend nursed me back, all the while reassuring me it was only a scratch. We laughed afterwards. Good times.

Debs and her friends returned mid morning. Now their sleeping bags and mats are strewn over the floor. After a tidy up, they join me for breakfast in the garden. Geraint and another Deborah had travelled most of the previous night to be here; they'd had two hours sleep before I heard them leaving. Andy and Catherine glow as they recall the sunrise and the power of the waves. Their chatter reminds me of when I was their age, though they are much better paddlers than me.

Andy asks if I still go out in my boat? Not often I tell him, explaining that the pull of family is hard to square with the demands of kayaking. He's a marine architect, working in Southampton, which he describes as 'not the best place for white-water', adding that his life is 'five days in the office then weekends on the motorway'. He talks eloquently of the tension between pursuing his career and a yearning for greater freedom, more time to pursue his dreams. It's a conflict I know well.

Geraint asks if I want to paddle that evening. I'd be fine he says, the skills would come back. Debs offers to watch me. 'We can go out at flat water,' she says, 'I'll stay close.'

I'm tempted to accept, to sod it all and take a chance. But then I weigh up the odds, think of the consequences and remember that it is the equinox. I'm touched by their generosity, but politely decline.

'Are you sure?' Debs asks, one last time.

I nod, and am happy with my choice, knowing that for me the tide turned a good few years ago.

Looking For Smoke Over Arnold's Hill

Three miles from my house is the largest starling roost in Wales. Every night between December and March up to three million birds gather on the south slope of Plumstone Mountain. A recent BBC film described it as one of Britain's natural wonders, and yet I had lived here for thirteen years before I found it.

In a sense this is not surprising, for to call Plumstone a mountain is a triumph of hope over strict definition. Separated from the Preseli ridge, too far inland to be considered part of the western headlands, Plumstone is little more than an incline on the road from Haverfordwest to Fishguard. Its summit is an oozing bog, crowned with an erratic boulder that marks the edge of the glacial advance that once covered Wales.

Even finding the roost wasn't obvious. I twice confirmed its location from a bird watching website but each time I went I saw only a few flocks. It was my third visit before I realised the starlings weren't heading to the summit; instead they flew to a small copse of trees that surround a rendering factory. It was an inauspicious location for such a significant gathering.

I'd often noticed the starlings in the fields at the back of my cottage. As the winter sun neared the horizon they would rise above the hawthorns, swirling into loops and curls, dipping and roiling in the sky. I would watch their elaborate dance, fascinated by the synchronicity of so many birds. Then suddenly their pattern would break and they'd head east in a rush of wind and wing beats.

But beyond those moments I'd given them little thought; starlings were commonplace, scrawny raiders of my bird feeders, bordering on vermin.

It was only after I read Mark Cocker's *Crow Country* that I began to wonder where they roosted. Cocker had become obsessed by the colonies of rooks near his home in East Anglia. His book describes his quest to understand their gregarious behaviour, and how, in so doing, he came to learn more about himself and his love of the natural world.

I read Cocker's book in the wet summer of 2008, confined to the house with a bad back and bleak temperament. There are rooks in my village, a dozen or so nest in the churchyard. I studied them over the summer, making mental notes of their departures and return, learning how they gathered in the fields before rising to trees at sunset. But by the autumn the young had fledged and the adults gone. I wasn't sorry; I had tired of watching and didn't miss their constant cackling.

The starlings were somehow different; their sheer numbers fascinated me. As my health and mood improved I found myself trying to count them, wondering why they made such efforts to come here each evening. Jane said they were like me, always wanting to return – to the same places, the same people, the same past.

'Look for the smoke over Arnold's Hill,' he said.

As I peered at the horizon a grey plume rose into the evening sky.

'That's miles away.'

'They'll be here soon enough,' he declared, 'from Milford too.' He pointed his stick toward a hen harrier that was circling over the trees, its ringed tail, long and straight. 'It'll be a good show tonight.'

My guide that evening was John. He farms much of the mountain and I knew him vaguely as a friend of a friend. I'd been so intent on watching the starlings arrive that I'd missed the welcome party that was gathering beyond his ramshackle barns. Half a dozen raptors were hovering above the hedges, thirty yards in front of the wood.

The first starlings flew in low, a group of a few hundred, heading straight for the trees. The next wave took a higher route, dive-bombing the copse. A third wheeled above the field overwhelming the raptors with speed and numbers.

More squadrons arrived. From Llanrhian, said John, from Preseli, Fishguard, St David's too. The sky was running with birds, the fir trees heavy with their silhouettes, their chatter like running water – a waterfall even.

As the gathering increased in size they stayed longer in air, circling above the copse in a slow promenade, the raptors now bystanders. I walked towards the trees, my heart racing, and as the sky darkened I realised I was standing in the shadow of a million birds.

And so began my own obsession.

That winter I would visit the roost whenever I could. If I was working away I'd go before coming home. As the light faded I'd dash through the lanes to John's farm, clocking the buzzards on the telegraph poles, glimpsing the boats off Skomer, always hoping for a sunset.

The best evenings had steel skies and crisp air. I was told that in these conditions the radar at Brawdy airfield could track the lines and even calculate the number of birds. December's frozen weeks brought an estimated two million each night, most of them travelling long distances to Plumstone.

This seemed incongruous. Why, when there must be thousands of alternatives, did they come to this particular spot? And why, when food is scarce, did they expend so much energy, only to face a gauntlet of raptors?

I read theories that speculated on a collective intelligence; others claimed safety in numbers, the gathering together for warmth. None of these was satisfactory.

'Bugger the theories,' said John. 'They come and that's all that matters. Some years it's millions, some years less – you'd never think they're a protected species.'

By the end of the winter I could look at the sky and anticipate how many there'd be. I learned to identify the columns, their direction and times of arrival; I knew the various hawks, which were likely to make a kill and which would flounder in the maelstrom.

But as February turned to March the arrivals were thinning, the sky less dark when they gathered. John explained that about half the birds are winter migrants; those that remain make for breeding grounds on the Pembroke peninsula. If I missed the black sky, he said, I should come at dawn when all the birds leave together.

The next morning there was frost on my windscreen.

I drove carefully through the lanes and parked by John's gate, noting the buzzard perched on the gable of his barn. The windows in his cottage were still dark, the curtains closed. There was no chatter from the trees; no sound of rushing water. I blew into my hands.

Moments later, the starlings began calling.

They cried weakly at first, a group at a time, as if they were gently waking each other. Gradually more joined the chorus, their collective calls like the off key note of a slide guitar. Except, instead of fading away, the noise grew louder and more insistent. It built to a collective scream; an urging to face the day.

Then it stopped.

And for a moment a shroud covered the sky and the early light was lost to their leaving. They were gone in less than a minute. It was like watching a film on rewind, the mass of birds breaking into columns, each heading in its own direction, getting thinner and paler the more I looked. A late sleeper left the trees in a panic; a sparrow hawk took it on the wing.

It was the last I saw of the starlings that winter. That evening I travelled to my house in Wiltshire. My work would keep me away from Wales and by the time I returned the roost was over.

If I describe the starlings to friends the response is always similar. There is mention of their flight, the swirling forms; comparisons to kaleidoscopes, oil on water, even Disney's Fantasia. It seems we are fascinated by their synchronicity; the apparently random yet tightly choreographed swarming, the swoops and falls and joy and delight of it all.

And most have a story to share. We're aware of starlings gathering in cities, under piers, on marshes and reed beds; one colleague talked of the flocks she'd seen on the American Plains. Starling roosts are a seasonal staple of television shows like *Spring Watch* and *Countryfile*. On the Somerset Levels they are promoted as a tourist attraction.

Yet when I listen to these reports they don't resonate. It took me a while to realise why, though the answer should perhaps have been obvious. We tend to view starlings from afar. Indeed any description of the swarming presupposes we are at a remove.

What I so loved about Plumstone was the opposite.

To visit the roost that winter was to be amongst the birds. At Plumstone the starlings fly over your head; on a heavy night they will literally touch your hair. There will be hundreds by your feet, on the wires and fences, more on the barns and hedges – drinking from pools, chattering on perches, flushed skyward by the raptors. There's a pair of resident goshawks that make their kills above the wooded break; a peregrine once stooped yards from where I stood, barrel rolling to clasp its prey from below.

Then there's the stream of chatter, and the overpowering stench of guano. Three months of a million plus birds and the copse stinks of sweet lime. If I walked in the trees I could stand under the roost, the sky reduced to starlight by the bursting branches, my boots sticky and my coat peppered with droppings.

The following summer I took to watching birds at the coast. I never did that list-ticking thing, though I'd often drive to Strumble to look for auks, or walk to St David's Head to watch the gannets diving off Ramsey. I liked best to go in the evening when occasionally there'd be shearwaters, flying low over the sea on their return to Skomer.

But all this was at a distance.

I missed the black shroud of the starlings, the closeness, the calling and the smell. By the following November I was back at Plumstone, looking for smoke over Arnold's Hill.

Except it didn't rise.

The flocks were back at the rear of my cottage and there were lines coming over from Llanrhian, but at Plumstone I could find only a few thousand birds.

'You're too impatient,' said John, 'some years they come in different waves.'

By December I was making nightly trips but the lines were only a little thicker. I sensed something wasn't right. One evening a family arrived to watch the spectacle and I advised them where to stand. 'Was that it?' the kids asked. I explained it was usually more of a spectacle, they should come back another night; I couldn't understand what had happened.

It was the raptors that gave me the clue.

As the family left I saw the female goshawk heading toward the north of the wood. To reach there would require a trek over the bog, so instead I sprinted up the track that comes out at the rendering factory. There is a clearing by its gates, which gives sight of the northern range of the trees.

You'd think that to miss two million birds might be difficult, and yet that's exactly what I'd done. They were gathering about as far from last year's roost as was possible at Plumstone. On a map it is no distance, but the limited access combined with the screening of the trees meant I'd spent four weeks looking on the wrong side of the wood. The starlings were coming from the east; they'd altered their flight paths so that John's farm was now the worst possible viewpoint.

Above the factory chimneys the birds were a roiling fish-ball, twisting into ever more intricate coils, splitting and regrouping, ebbing and flowing like the pull of the tide. The buzzards were ineffectual bystanders, the harriers much the same. It was, I think, a merlin that split the body of the show, about half the birds landing in a clap of wing beats.

Some twitchers arrived with binoculars and expensive looking telescopes. They ignored the starlings and, as is often the way with birders who visit the roost, asked me if any peregrines had shown.

From the clearing I could see more of the mountain; there were columns arriving from Preseli, from Fishguard and St David's – the sky was alive their surging patterns. I tried to get nearer the birds, but the ground was too soft and barbed wire blocked the way.

I didn't care; all that mattered was the starlings had returned.

That second winter brought more publicity to the roost. A BBC nature programme ran a feature, my own blog attracted much interest – I had people emailing from as far as Yorkshire, asking me the precise location, the best time to visit and the raptors that might be seen. One evening I took my neighbours, soon after they took their friends, who later took theirs. Some nights there were dozens of us there.

It wasn't entirely incompetence that had made me lose the roost; the birds were genuinely late that year and were coming in fewer numbers. But by January they were back in millions. John was happy they'd moved to the north side – less shit in his garden, fewer cars on his verge. The family who'd left so unimpressed returned with binoculars, video cameras, more kids than before. Coming to Plumstone was almost cool.

And yet to me that winter was a disappointment. The viewpoint had its advantages: I learned more of their patterns; the curving forms made for excellent photographs; I saw some spectacular kills. But my joy at finding the roost soon dissipated. The birds were a frustrating five hundred yards from the clearing. It was like watching on a screen; there was no sound of water, no taste of lime; no shadows in the gathering dark.

The roost was abandoned by March. In that year's glorious spring the migrants returned early and the residents moved to their breeding grounds. Plumstone was once again no more than a rise on the road to Fishguard. On the route to my village I'd often pass John's farm but never stopped.

At work, my colleagues consider me Welsh. If someone makes a joke about Wales they follow it with, *Sorry*, as if I might take offence. In fact, I first came here in my twenties and still spend half my life across the border. My job is based in Wiltshire, and though I no longer work full time my children go to school there and we're accustomed to a peripatetic lifestyle.

But my colleagues are correct in one sense. For it is me that longs to return, not Jane, and even less so my children, all of whom can claim a Welsh heritage. Often I go to back alone, spending long weekends writing and walking, especially in the winter when the surf has scoured the beaches and the estuaries are dotted with waders.

The following autumn was more difficult. We were moving house in Wiltshire. The new place was only down the road, but the process dragged and the change when it finally came unsettled me. Work was frantic too; September and October are the only months I work full time. For weeks there were workmen coming in and out, money consumed by one dubious necessity or another.

I took no joy in the house. My study was all wrong – poor lighting, not enough plugs – I couldn't write, I grumbled. We needed to go back home.

Jane said I was being irrational; the cottage would look after itself. We didn't need to make that trip every weekend, it was too costly and there were other priorities. By late December, we'd been away from Wales for the longest time in twenty years. I insisted we go back for Christmas.

When the day came, I packed the car with presents and went ahead of the others.

I arrived at the cottage to find dozens of droppings on the carpet, not unlike the body fluid that moths squirt if disturbed. Strange to find these in winter, I thought – and so many of them, on the windowsills, the cupboard doors, the bathroom sink. I noticed too, dusty marks on the ceiling and walls.

On the floor of our bedroom lay the body of the culprit. A starling had become trapped in the house, succumbing to lack of food or water – perhaps to panic. And it must have died recently, for the body was stiff and there was no smell of decay. I couldn't think how it got there: the windows had been closed, the post had gathered by the door; the neighbours would surely have left a note.

I held the bird by the window, the pearlescent blue and viridian feathers changing colour with the angle of the light. Its head was small, a dark green eye ringed with gold, and the beak longer and more elegant than I'd realised. The whole creature weighed no more than few ounces.

I carried the body to the garden and its wings opened one last time as I flung it into the field.

Half an hour later I stood under two million more.

No sooner had the starling hit the ground than I grabbed my keys and drove franticly through the lanes, racing the dying sun to Plumstone. The buzzards were gathering on the telegraph poles, the air over St Brides a grainy lilac, a tanker waiting in the bay.

John stood by his jeep, his stick resting against the fence. Nothing was said as I joined him. But I could smell the lime, and I noticed the road by his cottage was speckled with droppings, the trees stripped of their needles. The raptors hovered in the field as we looked towards Arnold's Hill.

And for thirty minutes the sky was black with their arriving: line after line, from Preseli and Llanrhian, from Milford and the south. At one point they were brushing our heads, the din of their chattering like the Gwaun in spate, the buzzards lost and pathetic in the bedlam.

I stepped into the road, held my arms upward and turned full circle.

'They're back,' I cried.

'They've come home,' John laughed. 'Pity about the shit.'

I stood there a few moments longer, imagining myself amongst them. After a while the roost settled and the raptors departed.

John returned to his garden. Did I want some cuttings, he asked?

I'd take some tomorrow, I said. Jane and the boys were arriving that evening. I had the fire to light, dinner to cook and the decorations to put up.

As I drove home through the lanes, the sun dipped behind Skomer and the late coming lines were streaks on a pink and purpling sky.

Amroth To Tenby

Today I went walking at Amroth. It's the start or the end of the Coastal Path, depending on how you look at it. My objective was Tenby, the most popular resort in Pembrokeshire and a town I'm never sure if I like. The walk between the two is one of the few sections of the path I've not completed.

My companion was my oldest friend – I was his best man and he was mine – twice! I hadn't seen him for eight years. Not that we had fallen out, it was more just kids, work, geography – all the excuses that make it easier to send a Christmas card with a promise to meet next year.

Our walk began in drizzle, a slate sea and no horizon. Amroth appeared closed for the winter, the rows of caravans covered in fallen leaves. It was much the same at Wiseman's Bridge – a pub with one customer, the cafe's billboard swinging in the wind, the one shop closed. These towns are not typical of the Pembrokeshire I love: they have concrete promenades, beaches with groynes and stone sea defences. Why choose to come here? I thought. But judging by the caravan parks, people do – and in their thousands.

Walking is good way to catch up with friends. The contours of the path give a rhythm to our conversation, talking and reflecting in response to its gradient. A lot happens in eight years, so I was pleased the going was easy. And as we chatted it was clear we'd both faired pretty well – not without incident – but not a bad outcome for two lads from the North. Our schoolteachers would be surprised I joked, mine especially.

As we approached Saundersfoot the wind picked up, a dinghy was making for shelter in the harbour. We stopped for tea in a chip shop and through the blurred window we watched the boats rising and falling on the swell. Ken reminded me of our motto when we were lads, 'if it rains, go the caff!' That still seemed about right.

Leaving the town the route steepens, making its way through pine and spruce woods, Tenby and Caldey in the distance. I began to like the path more; it has a gentle, almost subtropical feel to it, less demanding than the wilder north coast. I mentioned this to Ken and he replied that most folk would consider this fabulous scenery; 'you set very high standards,' he said.

Most of our chatter was about our children: their lives, their schools, what they like and hope to achieve – and what we aspire for them. Will they have our opportunities, I wondered? In some ways more – in areas like technology, travel, healthcare – but in others, they will need to strive harder – housing, pensions, careers. We agreed on this and many more of the concerns of two middle class, vaguely intellectual fathers, tramping the coast path in November.

Our arrival at Tenby came quicker than I expected; we passed the ugly apartments on the south promenade and made our way to the Georgian old town. After a pint in a forgettable pub we strolled round the centre, galleries and designer stores, side by side with ice cream parlours and pound shops. The contrast is common in Wales (in Aberaeron, for example) and generally I like it. But in Tenby the shops felt temporary, ill at ease in their surroundings; for all its heritage, the town seemed as if it didn't quite know what it wanted to be. Perhaps it's a seasonal thing.

I'd like to think that isn't like me or my friend. Despite an eight year gap we knew each other well enough to be at ease in minutes. And for all that we've travelled different roads, neither of us has changed very much: we retain similar values, similar goals, interests and outlook.

The sky was heavy as we caught a taxi back to Amroth – it had been twelve miles the driver said as I paid him thirty quid. It didn't feel as though we'd walked that far. Somehow, our journey seemed much shorter.

A taste Of Honey

As I drove past Newgale this morning I noticed the campsite was full; across the pebbles, many of the campers had already staked out their patch of sand. Two miles further, at Nolton, the car park was overflowing, a queue of people on the slipway. Over the hill the boogie boarders were braving the early morning waves in Broad Haven bay. At the prospect of sunshine, the crowds were gathering at the honey pots of the west.

On their day I like all of these places, though I'm not a great one for crowds – not one for sitting on the beach if I'm honest – so I was off to complete another section of the coast path. This time I was walking from St Martins Haven to Dale, a fiddly place to get to, which perhaps explains why it's one of the last sections I needed to complete. My plan was to drive to Dale, leave my bike, drive on to St Martins, park at the National Trust, walk the twelve miles of coast, cycle back to the car... you get the idea.

But sometimes the effort is worth it. A mile into my walk and I was above Marloes Sands, a kestrel above me and butterflies rising from the grass with every stride. Though it was the beach that held my gaze. I kept thinking, how could it be, that in all the time I've lived in Pembrokeshire I've never been here on a sunny day? The truth is, it's a faff to get here and there are easier options; much the same reason as why the crowds gather at Newgale.

On the headland at Hopper's Point I met a lady admiring the view. She told me she lived in Marloes and came here every day. 'Is there a better beach anywhere than this?' she asked. I had to agree. 'Not so many trippers come here,' she said,' because they have to walk four hundred yards from the car – that's fine for the rest of us though.' Again, I agreed. But when I asked if she'd been to Ynys Barry near Porthgain she said, 'Where's that?' And when I explained it was only a few miles to the north, she replied, 'You know, we never go to the north coast, it's terrible really.'

But talking to anyone was an exception today. I passed no more than a dozen people in as many miles. Every so often I'd come across a cove with sunbathers and perhaps a yacht off shore. There were farmers turning the fields, flocks of gulls crowding behind the tractors. The lighthouse at St Anne's was deserted; it's automatic these days. There were butterflies to spot too: Red Admiral, Painted Lady, Peacock, Comma, Common Blue, Meadow Brown, Wall, Small and Large Heath, Speckled Wood, Small White, Green Veined White, Grayling – and best of all, over a hundred Large White feeding on a bramble patch. Sadly, not one Tortoiseshell, which used to be so common only a few years ago.

The coast path turns north then east after the lighthouse, following the Daugleddau towards Milford Haven and Pembroke Dock. It's reputedly one of the deepest natural harbours in the world – on a day like to day it is hard to imagine such a wide passage could be dangerous – yet fifteen years ago the Sea Empress foundered off this headland, resulting in Britain's worst oil spillage. I remember the gulls washed up on Whitesands and the diggers scooping oil off the beach.

It would take a mean spirit to say the estuary was without beauty. Even the refineries seemed almost in keeping. It made me ponder if I'd ever come to accept wind farms quite so readily. My doubts were confirmed as I passed under the signal towers - there is something about getting close to these structures that brings home how out of place they are. Not that I have any alternatives to offer, especially if they save lives and help avert another spill.

My walk finished at Dale. The last time I was here was in winter – to look for birds on the River Gann – and I wondered then why it was so popular with summer visitors. As I walked down the hill, a hundred or so yachts came into view – each tied to its moorings, with easy access by pontoons in the sheltered bay. There were dozens of sailing types outside the pub, many more sunbathing on the harbour walls – they were laughing and relaxing, no rush to go on the water.

And why not, I thought, we each of us have our hefts – and it would be a shame if they were all the same.

Laughing at The Sky

A raven harries a crow. The Cheviot in billows of cloud.

Fragments, scribbled in a guidebook, yet a memory so vivid I could almost be back.

Back as a young man, on any of the countless days I sought escape there.

The rock smells of peat.

And back, twenty years later, sitting above a windswept crag and laughing at the sky.

It was a pilgrimage of sorts.

I wanted to visit the cliffs where I'd learned to climb; a homage to my youth that I'd planned for months, for years even. It would be nostalgic, a chance to unwind, maybe see some old faces – and I could write about it too, it would make a good assignment for my course. By September, everything was sorted: the time off work, my kit down from the loft, the guidebook found on a dusty shelf…

And then a message to say my father was dying.

I'd not seen him in twenty years, not since I'd moved to Wales in the Eighties.

The reason wasn't distance.

My father was a manic-depressive. As a child I'd learned his shift pattern so I knew which days were safe. My earliest memory is recounting them like a poem to help me sleep: *two till ten, six till two, two till ten, then night shift.*

I was a teenager when I understood that my father was mentally ill, but I remained in constant dread of his next outburst. It was only as a young man that I fought back, facing my fear, and learning to take control. By the time I left for Wales it was I who held the power between us.

And in the twenty years since, our only contact had been the birthday cards I allowed him to send to my boys – grandchildren he would never meet.

Jane, said I ought to see him on my way north.

I wasn't so sure. We'd reached an uneasy peace. Why risk it, after all these years?

'You know why,' she said.

A raven harries a crow.

The sun filtered over the moor as I walked to the crag. My trainers squelched in the peat and my ankles prickled from the heather that lined the path. Behind me were the great castles of the Northumbrian coast: Bamburgh, Dunstanburgh, Lindisfarne. But I was heading westward. As I neared the last rise I felt in my pocket for the guidebook but couldn't find it.

I ran the last few yards.

And there it was: a forty-foot high wall of pinking sandstone, immense against the steel blue sky. It was steeper than I remembered. And I'd forgotten the velvet lichen that coats the lower face, the copper streaks where the rain funnels from the moor, and the bracken that carpets the base. The salt smell of it too.

I had first come here when I was sixteen; skiving off school I'd hitchhiked the forty miles from Newcastle with a pal. My friend, a 'proper climber' who owned a rope and rock boots, had dragged me up a few of the easier climbs. It had terrified me, and I spent the afternoon looking over the moor, worrying how we'd get home and what I'd say if we were caught.

But I never forgot the exhilaration of that day.

And five years later, when my first job took me to live in Northumberland, I moved to a village in the lee of the moor. After work I would walk to the crag and watch the local climbers, envying their power and control. In the months that followed I made friends, bought some kit, and learned to climb myself.

For seven years this place was the fulcrum of my life. The first I spent strengthening my body and controlling my fear; the six that followed I tested them on increasingly difficult routes. My hopes, my friends, my future wife – all were connected in some way to those days. At night I would fall asleep to a mantra of climbs from the guidebook: *The Scorpion, The Scoop, Third Leaning Groove…*

The first face was drying in the morning sun.

I ran my hands across the rock, caressing the holds and sensing the dew that clung to its pumice like skin. A thin crack oozed with damp and I slipped my fingers into the fissure. I used to free climb this as warm up.

As I scanned the line, the sequence came back: jam the crack, feet to the break, twist and reach for the jugs. It was more of a boulder problem than a full-blown route.

'You go left from there,' a voice called from behind a boulder.

'I know,' I replied.

The first moves were thin, nubbins little bigger than my nails. My feet searched the wall for friction, forearms tightening as I pulled upward. There was a pinch and a lay off to the break. It felt awkward, my fist time on rock for how long? I reached high to the left, sinking my fist in a horizontal crack, feeling the grit bite on my knuckles.

The jam felt secure and I eased backward, humming the Eddie Grant song we used to play on the ghetto blaster: *I don't want to dance, dance with you…*

And then I fell off.

The jam gave way, my foot skipped and I clawed at the rock before landing on my arse. Blood oozed from my elbow and a sharp rock pressed into my lower back.

'Fuck it.'

'Told you it's easier to the left,' the voice called again from the boulder.

'I know,' I snapped.

'Canny-on. I thought you were new.'

'Returning,' I said.

'That's hard in trainers,' he continued. 'The trick's to avoid the crack.'

I limped to my rucksack and I saw him for the fist time. He was stripped to the waist, muscular and sun tanned – about mid twenties with a cheeky grin and spiked red hair. He stood up and tossed me his guidebook.

'There ye go'. He was wearing only boxer shorts, which had a lurid leopard-skin print. It was strange, I thought, to be changing here and not in the car.

The guide was a new edition: panoramic photos, overprinted with dotted lines. The climb wasn't marked – it never will be – for it's not a recognised route. No matter, I knew it from memory.

Climb directly, avoiding the crack and all easier options, then boldly to the top – preferably without falling.

It had been September – my father had phoned, spitting fists and threatening to 'have me out' because I'd challenged him for stalking my mother. I cut him off and went to the rocks. On my first attempt I'd fallen, succeeding the second time with what I thought was a badly swollen ankle. It was fractured in three places.

'I remember,' I smiled, and handed him back the guide.

*

Fifty yards to the north the cliff is undercut at the base, a popular place for friends to dump sacks and gather for some banter. The climber who had spoken to me earlier was there too. He was sitting on a boulder, drinking tea from a flask and making wisecracks to a lad climbing above him. He was still wearing only the boxer shorts.

I walked a little further and sat on a slab to put on my climbing shoes.

The rubber was brittle and the canvass uppers were spotted with mould after years of festering in a sack. I pulled the laces – they snapped. I retied them and squeezed my toes into the pointed ends – it hurt to walk. I clipped a chalk bag to my waist and wandered over to The Scoop – still couldn't find the guidebook.

The climb gets its name from a shallow groove that arches across the steepest part of the face. I recalled that the crux was more a test of nerve than strength, a bold move requiring friction and counter balance. And I reasoned the difficulties were low down – there was a patch of soft turf to jump to if it all went wrong. I dipped my hands in the chalk and pulled gently on a brittle flake.

The holds sloped more than I remembered but the boots felt better than trainers. I moved again; an undercut, a delicate step. It was steeper now, but still no problems. Another few pulls and I could cross to the scoop.

As I climbed a boy and his girlfriend arrived.

The girl uncoiled their rope. She spread it loosely on the ground, covering the soft turf that I'd planned to jump to as an escape route.

The boy started climbing beneath me.

I craned my neck as if to casually examine the next moves. A bridge to the scoop then the difficulties eased.

The boy was closer now.

My legs began to shake, involuntary tremors that are common with beginners. I pressed on my heels to stop the sewing machine action of my calves. One move, and the route would be all but over.

The boy was trying to climb past me.

I muttered to him under my breath.

'You've lost your sole,' his girlfriend shouted.

I wasn't sure if she was talking to me.

'Sorry, don't know your name. But the sole's fallen off your shoe.'

I looked down and saw the rubber last of my climbing boot amongst the bracken.

'No wonder it felt so hard,' I bluffed.

The boy let out a sigh, reversing the wall and stepping effortlessly to the ground.

I tried to follow but my fingers screamed too loudly, the rand on my boot was flapping and I could feel myself peeling from the face.

I jumped to the uncoiled rope.

Have you ever heard an old song on the radio and found yourself singing along as the words come flooding back? Each line flows to the next, verse following verse as the music triggers your memory. By the end of the song you're smiling and you wonder how you'd ever forgotten.

I had wanted my return to be something like that.

Climbing might appear as intuitive movement, but most often it is a well-practised choreography: the order of holds, the direction of pull, the intonation of balance. It has a level of particularity too that is hard to convey. I once sat in a pub with a stranger discussing a climb called Kipling Grove (so called because it's 'ruddy-ard') – should you pull on the flake or use it as an undercut? The hold in question is an inch wide and a thousand feet up the Langdale Valley.

Twenty years ago, every route, every hold on this crag had been burned to my memory. I knew the harder climbs would be beyond me, but I had planned on picking up the rhythm, finding my way in tune with the rock.

And if I could do that anywhere I wanted it to be here. For it was at this crag, this castellated wall, that I had learned to control my fear, and in so doing found a new form of freedom. I wanted to relive that feeling; to touch again those imperceptible moments that had changed my life.

But the melody was all off key.

I was too old, too stiff to do the moves.

And there was a lingering discord I hadn't counted on: a lament for a past that could never return, or a reminder that some things don't change?

The girl coiled the rope that was tangled in my legs.

'Are you alright,' she asked. 'You look a little white.'

I vomited on the grass.

'Too much Broon Ale?'

A voice quipped as it ran past me, not stopping for an answer.

A peal of laughter came from the overhanging wall to my left.

More climbers passed; a group of lads. They were running too, shouting and hollering as they gathered near the Wave.

The Wave is a smooth bronze wall, capped by a bizarre and striated overhang that resembles the filter flukes of a whale. It's an astonishing feature, the sediments laid down in flash floods and hardened over millennia until a fracture in the earth's crust revealed them to the sky. University field trips regularly come to view it, and climbers dream of the routes that breach its occasional weakness: *The Manta, Rough Passage, High Tide...*

One of the lads was using a video camera. Someone was trying to wrestle it from him. There was more laughter, a good-natured scuffle.

I walked over, spitting the taste of vomit onto the path.

Then a cry from above and a roar from the crowd.

The climber who had spoken to me earlier was traversing a wall. He had no ropes, no harness and no clothes – save for a g-string and the leopard skin boxer shorts that he now wore like a pirate's hat. A chalk bag was clipped to a cord round his waist.

Someone shouted, 'This is so going on You Tube.'

'Then get a good shot of me bollocks,' he replied.

'We'd need a more powerful zoom!'

He climbed quickly, assessing each hold then confidently executing the move – never looking down or back. At the break in the overhang he reached for the lip. And for few seconds he held himself over of the void, dipping a hand in his chalk bag and patting his groin.

'I need some more on me left one,' he joked.

Then he heel-hooked the bulge, swung his bare arse over the thirty foot drop and pulled smoothly to the top.

'He's a mad bastard,' said one of the crowd, shaking his head and chuckling.

Seconds later the climber was posing above the wave, flexing his muscles like a body builder, waving the shorts in the air.

The lads ran to the end of the cliff and the laughter faded.

I sat for a moment, trying to make sense of what had happened, grinning at the absurdity of it all.

There was more shouting from above; people laughing. The boxer shorts were thrown from the crag.

I could still taste the vomit from before.

As I rummaged in the sack for a water bottle my old guidebook fell from the pocket. The cover was faded, a black and white photo of a climber on a sharp arête, his rope arcing into the wind. Sand fell from the spine as I flicked through the pages.

And there, scrawled in the margins, in biro, pencil and marker pen, were the records I'd kept; notes and sketches, names and dates I'd not seen for twenty years.

Epic stories, captured in minimal form.

The Scoop: harder than it looks.

Comedies I'd forgotten.

Main Wall: fell off four times!

Days when nothing else seemed to matter.

The Viper: at last!

And other times too.

The day we lost Lucky in a rabbit warren; the Eat Again Café and the Belford Pie Shop; that midsummer's eve, so pissed I lost the tent.

It hadn't all been about power and control, some great coming of age that was defined by overcoming fear and facing out my father. It was about laughter too, about friends and joy, and evenings when I sat and watched the sun dip behind the mountains.

I had loved this place for what it was.

And it all came back – like the lyrics to a song.

The Cheviot in billows of cloud

At the far end of the cliff, the face eases into a series of black slabs. The wind has rounded the ledges and pink heather grows where few climbers venture. From here the moor undulates down to the spruce woods at Lowick, the field plain and the dunes at Lindisfarne.

The last route is Evening Wall, one of the easiest on the crag.

I traversed the slab, taking a diagonal line that ascends above a small cave. The sun had warmed the rock and I moved quickly to the ledge at half height. I brushed sand from the break and considered my position.

Above me, the face steepened, the holds no more than soft curves, the ledges damp and seeping. I was wearing one and half rock boots, and the sole of my 'good' foot was peeling too. A patch of bracken obscured the landing.

I stepped up.

The slab bulged and I leaned inward, seeking the false security of a closer contact. I felt exposed, the urge to down-climb fighting with a counter desire. I thought of my father, his angry, pleading eyes; I was here to remember the past, not to confront it.

Another step up.

My face was touching the rock. I sucked at the air, the taste of sand and heather mixing with the dry chalk from my hands. I thought of Jane, and my boys; how much they'd given me.

One more step.

The wind was cool and the air suddenly silent. I was poised on a sandstone slab, friction and fear holding me from a thirty-foot fall. And yet I felt calm, calmer than I had for years.

The last move is a grunt.

Arms, stomach, knees; they hauled me upward, until I half flopped, half rolled into a shallow puddle on the summit ledge.

The rock smells of peat.

I lay there a minute, the water creeping into my shirt, my eyes closed and the rhythm of my heart returning. A

126

skein of geese passed overhead and their honking calls carried me westward.

I opened my eyes to a wide Northumbrian sky.

And suddenly began to laugh.

Burbage

We're at Burbage Edge, first thing on Saturday morning. It's bitterly cold, the palest of blue skies, heavy clouds scurrying over Edale. A slow trickle of walkers leaves the lay-by, the collars of their jackets pulled high.

We walk down the track, passing the climbers huddled under Triangle Buttress. They're uncoiling ropes and blowing into cupped hands. The path is sodden, the puddles mirroring the sky as the sun brightens and the bracken glows a chestnut glory.

I feel an acute sense of my past, as if every step is one I've taken before: the mud squelching; the old millstones sinking and abandoned; the trickle of the stream as it runs underfoot.

As the track passes beneath the cliff that climbers call Burbage North, I strike up the hillside and call to the others to follow. Dylan is whingeing with the cold, but we cajole him on. 'Let me show you something,' I say. 'Something your Daddy did a long time ago.'

We clamber up the boulders, under stunted trees and over grassy ledges, to arrive beneath a steep buttress. The rock face is damp but it's drying in the sun; a fissure in the lower wall oozes green slime. 'This is Long Tall Sally,' I say, 'one of my better efforts.'

Mike looks at the blank slab and I explain how the route is climbed. It means little to him and in truth, I can't remember much, except a delicate blend of friction and bottle. I try the starting moves and get nowhere. Dylan tries to follow me up the lower ledge and I worry he will fall so I retreat ungracefully. By now the cold has crept inside our hats and coats.

We climb up the rough ground to the top of the crag. Jane gets stuck in a shallow gully, so I offer my hand and pull. We ought to go back, she says, if we turn now the wind will be behind us. I want to go on, further into my past, but I know the others don't share the enthusiasm. Dylan gives me a look that says 'carry please', so I distract him by saying that somewhere near here is a lion's cage; if he runs fast he might find it. He looks doubtful, 'You're tricking me again, aren't you?'

Nearer the road, there is raised boulder to our right, about twenty yards off the path. I head over, following a sheep track and stumbling as my boots catch in the heather. A grouse panics, flapping skyward as I hop onto the rock, look across the valley and turn – and there it is!

'It's the lion's cage,' I cry. 'I knew it was here; come and see, come and see.' Jane and the boys make their way to the boulder, still doubtful – I run ahead, eager to get there first.

The 'cage' is a square of iron railings that stands isolated on the moor. It is silhouetted against the now cobalt sky. I can feel my heart as I slow down for the last few steps and let the memories flood back.

Somewhere in my albums I have a photo of me and two old friends, growling and hooting behind the bars, pretending to be lions – or was it monkeys? It had been cold that day and none of us fancied climbing. I remember it took an age to set up the shot using a self-timer, and the walkers who passed us, staring as we snarled and screeched. I am laughing as I arrive, twenty-five years later.

The cage is no longer complete, the rusted gateposts unsteady to the touch, the bars twisted and flaking. But its basic structure is still there. I pick up a run of fallen railings and hitch its end over one of the iron spikes that remain standing, pressing the other deep into the peat – the new fence holds. Dylan runs over, 'Let me inside,' he calls, 'I want to be a lion too.' We chase each other round this strange edifice, jumping between the rails as Mike pretends to be a ringmaster.

I have no idea why the 'cage' was built here; it resembles the railings of a grave, but surely not? There's a deep hole in its centre – a flagpole or a mast perhaps? The iron was rotten when I first came, now it's barely holding together. Yet it retains a certain magic, a sense of incongruity in this bleak and beautiful landscape. The cage is beautiful in its own way too; the rust harmonious with the heather, the gritstone and the flurrying grouse.

We finish our lion playing game and walk back to the car. The others pile quickly inside as I search though the bags to find a camera. I run back over the moor to take some photographs, soaking my foot in a puddle as I crouch for a better angle and reel off a dozen shots before turning to leave.

A few yards further I trip over my laces and land with a face-plant in the heather. As I tie them again, the brackish water is squeezed from the cord, trickling over my fingers and into the peat.

Bleaklow

Bleaklow is not a place to walk alone. It's one of the darkest sections of the Pennine Way, a vast seething bog, a misty featureless plateau, a land for lost souls. Or so the reputation goes.

Saturday was cold, the sun struggling to break through. I parked at Snake Pass and set off into the wind – alone, save for a few sheep, watching me with that look of concentrated stupidity only they can muster. Best to get it over with I thought, pushing on up the hill. The path was mostly slabs, laid to prevent erosion of the peat – so much for a seething bog – in less than an hour I reached the Wainstones and Bleaklow Head.

On first impressions there's little here, even the peat has been eroded – a sad pole leans from the summit cairn. It feels lonely, not a place to linger, though by the numbers of walkers I'd passed it must be popular enough. I took off my coat and made for Torside Reservoir; if I kept my head down I might get there in an hour.

Just over the rise I noticed what I took to be a white rock in the peat hags; it seemed out of place amongst the gritstones. I looked carefully but couldn't it figure out; perhaps it was a bag left by the slab layers? On an impulse I plodged through the bog toward it. A few yards from reaching the stone, it moved – bounding over the hag and stopping to stare at me before hunkering down. It was a mountain hare!

I waited and another appeared – this one had lost its winter coat – then another, a white one this time, and another... I'd never seen hares on the moors before. They seemed untroubled by my presence, scampering about the hags, occasionally rising on their haunches for a better view. A group of walkers I'd overtaken below the summit passed me, perhaps wondering why I was standing ankle deep in the mire. 'There ain't now't much up there,' one of them called.

A little further and the path follows a stream, the water dribbling over slabs into a series of pools, fresh with weed and moss. I'm not sure how long I sat there, but I saw a dipper, a golden plover, two grouse, some wagtails, a hawk in the valley below. I drank some water from the pool and feasted on a hot cross bun.

From Clough Edge I mentally traced the line over Black Hill, the next section of the Way. The wind was whipping up horses on the reservoir; I saw the walkers making their way on the lower path. Coming down the ridge I met a National Park Volunteer. He asked about my walk and we talked about the slabs that he claimed had encouraged more visitors. 'It's a peculiar thing,' he said, 'folk tend to do this walk in groups, but it's always the lone walkers who see the most.'

He confirmed it was a dipper and a probably golden plover that I'd have seen. I told him about the hares. Did they still have their winter coats, he asked? Magnificent, we agreed, and he hurried to look for himself.

An hour behind schedule, I walked the shore of the reservoir to meet my lift at Crowden.

Doethie

Often it's the snatched opportunities we remember most. Trips planned too carefully can easily fail our expectations, leaving us deflated and wondering why we made the effort. When I think back it's the chance encounters that are vivid in my memory.

And so it was last weekend. I'd planned to go backpacking with Daniel, mapping a trek over the Beacons, researching wild campsites – I'd even packed his rucksack. 'I don't fancy that route,' he said, as we're about to leave. 'It's too far and too high, can't we go somewhere different?'

We'd already had a row – over his teenage lounging as everyone else was getting about the morning. It was midday and I was keen to be off. 'We could go to the Doethie,' I suggested, 'though it's a bit of a drive.'

'Excellent,' he replied, 'I can sleep in the car.'

The Afon Doethie rises in the southern hills of the Elenydd, falling steeply into the wider curves of the upper Towy at Llandovery. The Towy is a favourite with picnickers, who splash in the shallows to the annoyance of fishermen casting lines into stilling pools. A few miles upstream the Doethie Valley marks the end of the road, the only way on by foot or horseback. At its head, only five miles distant, the valley joins the high plateau above Soar y Mynydd chapel and the Llyn Brianne dam. Anyone wanting to be picked up there would need a driver prepared make a twenty mile diversion round the watershed.

We started our walk above Rhandirmwyn, it was late afternoon by then and I was hoping to camp by a copse of oaks at the bottom of the valley. As we neared I noticed there were two jays in the trees; they were very unsettled, screeching *kraaws* as they flew nervously between the branches. It was too early to stop, so we carried on, reaching the track to Soar y Mynydd as the sun neared the hills. From here we walked to the old youth hostel at Tyncornel, once an isolated farm accessible only by the drove road from Llanddewi Brefi. I love this place, rescued from closure by the Elenydd Trust it is the remotest hostel in Wales. The volunteer wardens, Mark and Bronwen, greeted us. Would we like a cup of tea they asked, and why don't we camp in the garden?

The hostel has a snug with an open fire, there's one conversation and you either join in or slink off. And as so often happens in these places you realise it's a small world. Bronwen was studying creative writing, so we talked of tutors and assignments; and when I said we had come from Pembrokeshire Mark told me how he and a friend had once walked four miles to a pub inland of Solva only to find it had closed the week before. That pub is next door to my house, and I vaguely remember two parched blokes sitting on the wall, and their disappointment as I told them they'd wait a long time if they wanted a pint.

As we returned to the tent the night was sparkling with stars; I could see the Andromeda galaxy, the Milky Way a band from black mountain to mountain, the occasional meteor falling through Leo. The tent was thick with dew, and we snuggled into our bags leaving the door open to the sky. 'I like it here,' Daniel said, falling immediately to sleep.

Next morning we packed and ate breakfast with our new friends; a woodpecker joined us on terrace, picking at the nuts in a feeder. Some of the hostellers were walking to Dolgoch, the other hostel rescued by the trust – it is lit by gas and has a church organ in the sitting room. But we had to retrace our steps, descending with the river to the car.

It was swift walk, not a cloud, the bracken damp and smelling of earth; two ravens sat by the oak trees where we'd seen the nervous jays. Daniel strode ahead, leaping over the pools and dew soaked ground; his back as broad as mine, his body chiselled and hard. The river, young too at this height, cascades over rocks and falls, foaming and gouging in its haste to reach the flatter land.

I walked the last miles behind Daniel, enjoying the silence, the company of the water. As I stopped to drink a dragonfly rested on my arm, its huge eyes watching, as if daring me to move. It followed me a while, attracted by the colour of my rucksack, until I reached the road at Troedyrhiw farm.

Daniel was waiting at the car, lying on the grass and looking at the sky. We had parked near the cave of Twm Shon Catti, the Welsh Robin Hood. Legend says he took shelter in these hills before building a manor at Tregaron and becoming a pillar of society. I wonder if he ever returned – snatching a visit on days when the sun shone and the Doethie tumbled through the autumn bracken, jays in the oaks and dragonflies over the pools.

I expect he did – for there are few finer places in Wales.

The White Tower

On the low sloping cliff to the north of Porthgain is a white tower. It is made from fieldstone, about the size of a small kiln, mortared with mud and lime. The tower is one of two markers that indicate safe passage to the harbour. A few years ago its starboard sister was struck by lightning, I'm told. The locals rebuilt it, for in a heavy storm the fishermen need these towers still.

I walked there yesterday, alone on a December morning. I'd forgotten a scarf, my ears sore in the wind. As I climbed the sticky mud path a flock of curlew flew from the sand by the slip; they rose to the crumbling walls of the hoppers that loom over the quay. The hoppers, a relic of Porthgain's industrial past, once stored the graded rocks that were loaded onto sloops bound for Liverpool and Newport.

Looking north, I felt the curve of the ocean folding over my shoulder. The light at Strumble was flashing and I could make out Pwll Deri hostel beneath Garn Fawr, *the big cairn*. Yesterday the sea was flat, a gunmetal grey darkening to a pewter horizon, lobster pots bobbed in the marbled swell. I have stood here, in other Decembers, drenched, as the waves swallow the cliffs and clots of spume settle, as if it were snow, on the dun grass.

In the lee of the stack I thought of the times I have come here; the years of looking, of painting the view, counting boats... I remembered too, our boys running round it and how Jane said it was the magic tower – five times for luck, five more to earn a wish. They used to hold their coats above their heads, leaning and screaming into the breeze.

As I made to leave I had a sudden urge to measure the tower's circumference; holding my arms at full stretch I sidled round, hugging the pock marked stones. Its girth is four and half spans and I have the whitewash on my fleece to prove it. Two gulls were circling above; they were black-backs, dismissive of the kestrel that hovered in the ridge lift, its tail held flat for balance, down and into the wind.

The tower is one of my returning places; one of six or seven locations to which I'm repeatedly drawn. These are not large areas such as Pembrokeshire or the Elenydd, though my delight in those landscapes means I visit them more than most. My returning places are specific, somewhat peculiar, not in the tourist brochures. They are places I come to, as if in ritual; places that hold significance I don't fully understand.

My family joke about it.

Can't we go somewhere new, they say; the older boys suddenly have homework, friends to visit or arrangements that couldn't possibly be broken. Increasingly I go alone. Last year I drove four hundred miles to a windswept crag. For an hour I sat in the bracken between the sandstones and watched geese flying south. Then I drove home.

'Nostalgia is heroin for old people,' my eldest son ribbed me this Christmas. He has the confidence of youth and a healthy dismissal of his father's habits. When his girlfriend first came to our house, he advised her, 'Don't talk to my Dad, he's a bit weird.' It was she who told me this, as she teased him for his similarity to me. I reminded him too, of the hundred mile journey he'd made to be with her on their anniversary.

'That's wasn't nostalgia,' he replied, and I'm sure he's right. He's right too, that I have a tendency to reminisce. I can spend hours flicking through the albums in my study:

pictures of me as young man, of Jane who so besotted me, of my boys asleep as toddlers, their arms intertwined.

But he's wrong to assume my visits to the tower are merely nostalgic. For the sea is too close, the wind and the surge too immediate. In places like this our senses are alert. We feel part of it, truly alive – and yet we feel small, insignificant even. No more able to escape the cycle of growth and decay, than are the cliffs, the waves, or the kestrel hovering in the wind.

On my way back to the car, I looked across the harbour to other tower. It is higher than mine and not so white; for the first time I noticed its top was shaped to a fine point, resembling a sharpened pencil. It struck me that in the twenty years I have been coming to Porthgain, I have perhaps been to that tower twice. This is strange, for it stands less than fifty yards off the path to Aberieddy, a walk I know intimately.

The path takes the steps by the pilot house where it meets the old tramway. The track is sunken into the land, a sort of hollow way that emerges at the quarry where choughs nest and I saw my first Clouded Yellow butterfly. Round to the west are the headland fingers of Penclegyr, which create the tidal rip off the beach at Ynys Barry. Not long after I first came here, a father swam to his son who was struggling in the ebb. The son made it to shore; the man's body was found in Cardigan Bay.

There were white horses that day. I remember because I'd arranged to go surfing with a friend and was checking the waves when the maroon went up. I returned to find his car gone and was furious that he'd buggered off, before someone told me he was on the lifeboat. 'He could have said,' I moaned – I was like that then.

When Jane was first pregnant we'd often walk on that beach; once we found an abandoned seal pup, bloodied from the storms, and wondered if its mother would return. Jane asked if I thought I'd give my life for a child of my own. My reply was cold, a philosophy on the relative value of adult and infant lives. She reminds me of that sometimes.

I was thinking of this as I drove home, stopping to see my neighbour, the artist John Knapp Fisher. John is perhaps the finest landscape painter in Wales; for forty years he has lived and worked from his cottage-cum-gallery, two miles from the harbour. As we chatted I noticed a tiny watercolour of a bare field, the furrows white with snow, trees stark against a brittle sky. It was dated 1962 and the sticker said, *Not For Sale*.

'I painted it for my father,' he said. 'The strange thing is, I remember everything about that day: the smell of the field, the trees thick with frost. I remember the brush strokes, the colour of my water – the taste of paint on my lips.'

He peered closely, as if looking for the first time. 'Everything,' he said again.

I told John about my visit to the tower and how I'd noticed the other was pointed. He laughed. Of course it was, didn't I know anything about boats? If the towers were alike, then how would the fishermen know which direction to head? In poor visibility, the same shapes would be fatal.

I drove back to the harbour and looked again at the second tower. Its column was square not round, it was higher on the cliffs, and its colour much darker than the one I was so familiar with. I climbed the steps to get closer.

From the tower I looked toward Penclegyr. The sea was running north, white horses on the line of the rip. In summer, porpoises sometimes gather here as the fish are driven by the tide; its pull beyond the power of any swimmer. I tried to imagine what that father felt, drifting toward Cardigan Bay. He must have seen the towers; did he know his son had made it to shore?

As I walked to the edge I noticed the kestrel. It was facing inland, poised above the small patch of stones that separated me from the void. I moved forward and it stooped lower, its wings arched and upright, the black tips beating high above its head. And from somewhere long buried I remembered sitting with my grandfather in a scrub field by his house, describing for his milky eyes a hawk that had joined us.

Windhovers, he called them.

Occasionally, I will try to explain why I enjoy returning, typically after Jane has made an exasperated comment to guests who asked of our holiday plans. The charge is that I only visit the same old places, the implication that I'm wary of the new; that in a world of opportunity, I'm missing out.

And yet the hard facts suggest otherwise, for I have travelled widely to America, Asia, Africa – and not to the packaged resorts, which model their attraction on an excess of home comforts and a splash of sunshine. Of course, if your idea of somewhere new is a concrete hotel and the weekly barbecue at Smuggler's Cove, then I'm guilty as charged.

The new doesn't scare me, I say, but the point about returning, is that there is joy in familiarity. I might mention John the painter, who's found a lifetime of work within five miles of his home. *Dyner filltir sgwa*, they say in Wales: a man of his own square mile. And often when we see things again, they are all the more surprising; like the second tower yesterday.

But this seldom has any effect. I can sense the glazed expressions; the polite nods, before the inevitable jest that moves the conversation on.

What I don't say is that there are times in our lives when we transcend the everyday; when for an infinitesimal moment, and before we have classified the thoughts into time and place and logic, we see the world anew. These moments burn into our memories, changing us forever. And if nostalgia is a yearning to touch them again, then perhaps my son is right after all.

I took Dylan to the tower last summer. It was hot; we bought ice creams and walked under the hoppers to the end of the quay. He sat on the pier with the ocean to his back. There were shoals of blennies in the harbour, and a spider crab, one limb missing, climbing the wall. Dylan preferred the lime kilns and the iron ladders, the detritus of the quarry. How big were the boats and how were they loaded? Did they have sails? Are trams the same as trains?

There were midges at the tower, and Common Blues feeding on the thrift. Let's look for seals, I suggested, 'Mum would like that.'

'Let's play the talking game,' he replied.

The game is Dylan's invention; only he is allowed to speak. My role is to be whatever he asks – usually I'm a passenger, sometimes a fireman, and once, on the Mer de Glace under Mont Blanc, vultures circling on the thermals, I was promoted to engine driver. In the six years he has graced my life, Dylan has shown a comprehensive disregard of nature.

And yet being with him is one of my greatest joys.

You must be mad, our friends had joked. Weren't two boys enough? And how big was the gap: almost ten years? We had an accident once, someone confided. 'It wouldn't have been fair on our others, so… you know.'

We came to the tower when Jane was pregnant with Dylan. It was evening, the last light fading behind an inky sea. I sat with my back to the stones, my hands on her belly as she rested between my legs, 'We could make love here,' she teased, 'No-one would notice.' And I blew into her ear as we looked toward Strumble.

'Like we did that time,' I reminded her.

'That's enough,' she eased upward from my arms.

We returned to the harbour, toward the lights of the Sloop Inn. Water lapped at the slip, the stays and shrouds of the fishing boats chiming with the tide.

'Do you think we'll be all right,' Jane asked, 'doing it all again?'

My good friend Jim Perrin once spoke to me of the objective correlative in nature; I had to look it up. He was referring to the capacity of landscape to hold a mirror to our feelings, to embody our spirit in physical form. We return to certain places, he was saying, not so much to look at the view, as to look at ourselves.

And he should know. Jim lost his son to suicide and his wife to cancer, both in a year. Soon after, he returned to climb the Old Man of Hoy, a tottering sea stack in the Hebrides on which his son had suffered an accident that led to his depression. Returning was an act of pilgrimage. It was too, a confirmation of something he'd discovered: that through memory, in profound grief there can also be profound joy.

I cannot imagine Jim's pain, or conceive of the strength of his returning. But when I stand at the tower I feel something akin to that last contradiction.

Jane tells a story of how I was when we met. 'As nervous as a whippet,' she says. 'I thought I'd never get a decent night's sleep.'

'I never want to be tied down,' I had told her. 'Life's a tick list; I hate people who do nothing.' And that wasn't all. 'Children won't change me,' I'd said. 'Love's a chimera; ultimately we're all alone'.

For me, the tower is not so much a mirror, as a negative. What draws me there is that it doesn't change – or least it does so slowly – its immutability in contrast to the daily rush, to the getting on and what next and who's been promoted; to the putative heroes of outdoor pursuits; to the sub-life of work where the price of progress is a loss of self – to those things I once thought important.

The tower, in not changing, reminds me how much I have.

This morning I returned again; Jane was with me.

A storm had drummed the windows all night. Outside, the power lines were down, streetlamps flickering, the clouds heavy with showers.

'Who fancies some air?' I asked over breakfast.

We left the boys watching TV, Dylan issuing tickets for his railway and instructing his brothers not to talk.

Jane held my arm as we walked the path, the boats straining on their hawsers as a wave broke over the pier. A net had fallen from a deck and was spreading to the rocks, a herring gull pecked at its turquoise web.

At the tower, surf was engulfing the lower cliffs, the sucking of the ocean drowned by the sound of the wind. Every so often the sets would falter, and the rock doves would shuffle on their ledges to peer at the roiling. There was no horizon; I couldn't see Strumble or Pwll Deri.

Across the bay, towards the other tower were three spheres, ducking and rising in the surf.

'Are those seals?' Jane asked.

'They're buoys, I think; lobster pots probably.'

She put her arm round my neck and snuggled into my shoulder. 'That's a pity.'

'There was kestrel here yesterday,' I said. 'It came to the other tower later – as if it were watching over me.'

'You are strange,' she laughed. 'You see meaning in everything.'

'Do you remember,' I asked, 'how the boys used to charge round here, their coats above their heads?

'You'd stand by the cliff in case they ran too far.'

A wave clapped the rocks and a shower of spray fell on the tower. I kissed the salt on Jane's cheek then moved to the edge, leaning into the breeze.'

'And do you remember what they used to shout?' Jane called above the current.

I turned toward her, held my coat aloft and for an instant I was back there again.

'Feel the wind,' I cried. 'Feel the wind.'

A New Colour – An Afterword

Let me tell you how it feels.

I want you to imagine a new colour. Not a shade or hue mixed from those you know. What I want you to do is imagine an entirely new colour, as if the spectrum had suddenly expanded.

Try now and you'll understand me better.

The concept is easy enough. I expect you understood what I asked. Yet it was beyond you, beyond any amount of trying.

Now imagine a world where almost everyone but you sees this colour. They describe it as warm, or spicy, it makes you feel happy; you feel good about this colour, they say.

Is it any clearer now?

Once in a while I glimpse it – a sort of déjà vu.

But this is the closest I get.

So what follows are fragments – it is all I can offer.

This is how it feels.

It is the first time we've met.

The room is smaller than I expected: two chairs half facing each other, a low table with dried flowers and a box of tissues, a heater on the wall with a dial that she turns as I sit down.

She waits.

They always wait.

I know it is me who must start.

Eventually the words come, half spontaneous, half rehearsed – a lifetime squeezed into a few faltering sentences.

This will continue for months.

'We have a lot to do.' She smiles and I warm to her. We begin.

To see us walking together, you'd never have thought he was blind.

'We'll not go home yet,' he said, 'I've got something to show you.' He ruffled our hair and we walked him slowly down the street, past neat rose gardens towards the fields by the pit.

'How do, Seppy?' a neighbour called. 'With your two little soldiers, I see.'

He raised an arm, his hand bent inward, the twisted fingers locked like claws – arthritis had got him too.

The scrub fields by the old railway line were fenced off. There was a hole in the wire and we slipped through, guiding him by the hand as we walked down the cinder track, overgrown with hawthorns and bramble. 'We should be nearly there,' he said.

About eight feet up, in the crook of a stunted tree, we saw it. It was made from sticks, and lined with golden straw, big enough for a man, even two, to lie down in. We climbed up and rolled into its bowl, peering over the rim, sunlight dappling through the leaves.

'What is it,' we asked, 'What's it for?'

'It's a tramps nest,' he replied.

'Can we sleep here?'

'Not tonight,' he said, and he lay down on the grass to doze.

We stayed there an hour, perhaps two, pretending we were tramps, eagles on a mountain cliff, pirates at sea. We'd never seen anything like it: a whacking great nest in a tree; a tramps nest, he'd said.

How did he know it was there?

The sky was softening as we walked home, pylons casting long shadows on the allotments, birds gathering on the wires. In the last sunlight, dozens of bees were feeding on thistles that lined the narrow path through the field. They were head-high to us and we were afraid.

'Show me,' he said, bending low, his face inches from the bees. He felt for a thistle, cupping a hand under the purple heads. Gently, he coaxed a bee onto his fingers, letting it walk across the back of his hands, explore his swollen knuckles and crusty yellow nails. Raising his hand to his face, the bee crawled behind his glasses, past milky eyes and down his cheek.

Collecting it between twisted fingers he replaced it on the flower. 'You see,' he said, 'nature knows what will harm it.'

We held his hand through the fields and walked proudly with our grandfather past the neat rose gardens to home.

My father stood waiting in the passage, his tongue between grinding teeth. 'Upstairs, you two,' he said. He was wide-eyed and angry.

We dared not pass him.

'Now,' he snarled.

But Seppy held us close.

'Not one hand,' he said. 'You hear me, Neil. Not one hand.'

We were driving through Mid-Wales, and I noticed she wasn't wearing socks. Her legs were bent at ninety degrees, pale ankles showing between the hem of her jeans and the tan leather pumps that she had a habit of perching on the dashboard, passenger side.

She leaned back, her blouse open enough to show small breasts in a white bra. We'd been singing since Dolgellau, past Dinas Mawddwy to Llanidloes; laughing at our tuneless renditions of American Pie and The Boxer – forgetting the words.

As I looked at her white ankles and her slender feet in those tan pumps I knew.

I knew I wanted those same feet to be perched on my dashboard in another ten years; twenty years – more.

That evening, in Aberystwyth, in a hotel by the sea, she pulled on a pair of blue and white pants and tiptoed to the bathroom thinking I was sleeping. The wallpaper was brown with orange flowers, the en-suite had royal blue tiles and a fan that clattered – and I told her. I told her for the first time, and I meant it more than ever before; ever will again.

Later, when we first lived together in a small cottage in New Street, amid the mess of my divorce, the guilt and grief, my counsellor asked me, 'Who would you like to be the mother of your children?'

And in the instant before thought, I glimpse it.

I see her standing in that hotel room, the fan clattering – and those ankles, without socks, perched high on the dashboard, passenger side.

I twist the key, push open the front door, throw the laptop onto the hall table with little care and turn into the living room, exhausted.

They are sitting together on the sofa. The TV is playing without volume.

'Daddy,' they cry, 'Come and sit with us.'

I settle down between them and rub my hands through their hair, one soft as feathers, the other thick and wiry like mine once was. They curl beside me, balls of crumpled tissue, and I smell their fresh clothes as they snuggle into my arms.

'We missed you.'

'I missed you too,'

'Tell us a story.'

'Later,' I say, 'I'm very tired.'

'Please.'

'What sort of a story?'

'About when you were little; about when you were a boy'.

'I can't think. Not now anyway.'

'Tell us anything. We don't care if we've heard it before.'

So I tell them… *how we used to go to the sweet shop and ask for hot ice cream and polo mints without holes, and sports mixture from a jar on the highest shelf…. and just when Mr Newcombe was up the ladder, we'd scarper from the shop…* I run my fingers over their chests to show what scarpering means.

They laugh and twist with the tickling.

'Did Mr Newcombe ever tell the policeman?'

'My father was the policeman,' I say.

'But did he tell him?'

'I can't remember. It was a long time ago.'

'Tell us some more.'

'I haven't time,' I say.

But I don't leave. I feel the softness of their bodies, their frail arms in mine, the warmth of their breath, and I wonder what they're feeling. I watch them smiling as they look at me, believing every word.

'Tell us about Seppy,' says my eldest. 'Tell us that story about the nest you found.'

Tears fill my eyes.

'He was very kind,' I explain, 'And he'd have loved you very much.'

I hug them again and the glimpses fade quickly to black.

That night, in bed with Jane, I say, 'You know all those books we read when you were pregnant?'

'Yes,' she relies, sleepily.

'They never say they'll love you back.'

I cycled with him to the caff on Sunday morning.

It was raining but he wouldn't be put off. He wore a flimsy green waterproof over his tee shirt and rode the little bike I'd built for him with a steady ease and natural balance.

We rode slowly at first. I was nervous. 'Look for cars; watch the roundabout; stay left; keep in; I said stay LEFT!'

But soon we were chatting more easily – about the Tour de France, Lance Armstrong and the King of the Mountains; could he have a new bike for Christmas?

I rode behind him, the rain streaming off his waterproof, onto his wheel and into my face. I cycled in the middle of the lane; if a car comes too fast, I reason it can hit me first.

The old guys in the caff clapped him in when we arrived; twenty miles is a long way for an eight year old. To see his face when they did that.

We had beans on toast and he gulped a can of Doctor Pepper before Jane came to pick him up and I rode back alone to meet them at home.

That year I cycled 4000 miles. I once rode beneath two golden eagles, circling on thermals as a pale mist rose over Mont Blanc.

I would have swapped them all – every mile, every pedal rev – for that one glimpse, for that ride to the caff on Sunday.

She sits in her chair, smiling gently, hands on her lap. I fumble with my wallet and phone before settling down. The room is warm and now familiar: the coffee table with dried flowers, the box of tissues; the dial on the heater that she fiddles with every week.

It's always me that must break the silence.

'I went cycling on Sunday,' I say.

We exchange a few pleasantries about Jane and the boys, though she'll never meet them.

It has been this way for the last few months; not so much avoiding issues as a sign that they're worked through. I explain about the ride and how I felt.

'You've come a long way,' she says.

'I guess so,' I agree and I ponder my journey.

'When you first came here you said that being a father was like being given a map but no compass.'

'No reference points,' I correct her.

'That's right,' she says, 'But you have those now?'

'Some.'

I want to say more but the words don't come, until eventually. 'I'm worried, about finishing here. What if I lose my way.'

'Can't this be a reference point?'

'Not one I want to return to.'

'Not if you want it to end.'

'That's just it,' I say. 'I don't know what the ending will be.'

She smiles kindly.

'It will be the same as all your others.'

'Like a new colour, perhaps?'